Hands-On GEOGRAPHY

Grades 3-5

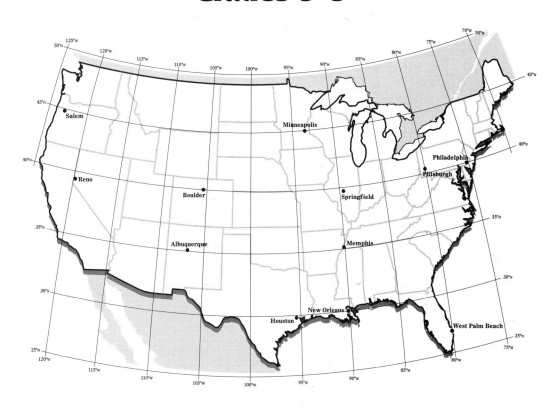

by Isabelle McCoy, MEd
& Leland Graham, PhD

Carson-Dellosa Publishing Company, Inc.
Greensboro, North Carolina

Acknowledgements

The authors of *Hands-On Geography* wish to acknowledge the following educators who provided suggestions and helpful comments in the preparation of this book: Coco Graham, Thomas McCoy, Ben Ridgeway, Stan Powell, Virginia Powell, John Spilane, Naomi Terry, and Connie York.

Credits

Editor:
Sabena Maiden

Layout Design:
Mark Conrad

Inside Illustrations:
Allana Kereluk
Bill Neville
Mark Conrad
Van Harris

Cover Design:
Annette Hollister-Papp

Cover Photos:
© Comstock, Inc.
© Dynamic Graphics, Inc.

ISBN 1-59441-183-2

Introduction

. studies suggest that geography has been a neglected subject. One possible
could be the emphasis that is placed on teaching the subjects of math, science,
ading. Research indicates that the amount of time spent teaching geography
fficient, resulting in students who are geographically "illiterate." Hands-On
aphy contains a variety of activities designed to increase students' interest,
edge, and awareness of geography.

aphy was once divided into two main categories: physical geography and
geography. Today, geography crosses over into other sciences, such as
al anthropology, demographics, economics, sociology, and zoology. Geography
better defined as a branch of science that includes all parts of the earth's
al features and populations. Geography includes the study of almost
ng about the earth, such as land, sea, and air features and the distribution of
, animals, and people. The list seems to be endless. The study of geography
erent from other sciences because it examines its topics from the view of
they are located and what relationship they have to the things around them.
nds-on activities in this book reflect the five themes of geography published
Guidelines for Geographic Education: location, place, human/environment
ction, movement, and regions.

cus of this book is not for students to simply memorize place names and their
ns around the United States, but rather to understand the concepts behind the
and to recognize the relationships between places in the country. The first
of the book contains activities that concentrate on strengthening map skills and
standing the five themes of geography. The second section of the book includes
on activities to reinforce a variety of geography concepts centered around the
States. The third section is comprised of charts, graphs, and diagrams that
ts will encounter on standardized tests. Finally, the appendix contains a variety
rics, graphic organizers, the National Geography Standards, and an answer key.

sted activities for the United States Map on pages 6-7:
ke a copy of the map for each student. Have students label each state, draw a
r for each capital city, color each state using different-colored pencils, and
el the significant bodies of water.
ke an enlarged copy of the map. Using different-colored markers, color each
te. Laminate the map. Place the map and a black, write-on/wipe-away marker at
ocial studies center. Provide time for each student to label the states correctly.
lude a smaller, labeled version of the map at the center for self-checking.
ke an enlarged copy of the map. Using different-colored markers, color each
te. With a black permanent marker, write each state's name. Laminate the map.
t out each state to make a puzzle. Place the map puzzle in a social studies
nter. Provide time for each student to assemble the states correctly. Include a
aller, labeled version of the map at the center for self-checking.

Table of Contents

Re
cau
and
is ii
Ge
kno

Ge
hun
cult
is n
phy
any
plan
is d
whe
The
in tl
inte

The
loca
nam
sect
und
han
Uni
stud
of ri

Sug
• N
  s
  l:
• N
  s
  a
  I
• N
  s
  C
  c
  s

© Ca

Table of Contents

Introduction

Recent studies suggest that geography has been a neglected subject. One possible cause could be the emphasis that is placed on teaching the subjects of math, science, and reading. Research indicates that the amount of time spent teaching geography is insufficient, resulting in students who are geographically "illiterate." Hands-On Geography contains a variety of activities designed to increase students' interest, knowledge, and awareness of geography.

Geography was once divided into two main categories: physical geography and human geography. Today, geography crosses over into other sciences, such as cultural anthropology, demographics, economics, sociology, and zoology. Geography is now better defined as a branch of science that includes all parts of the earth's physical features and populations. Geography includes the study of almost anything about the earth, such as land, sea, and air features and the distribution of plants, animals, and people. The list seems to be endless. The study of geography is different from other sciences because it examines its topics from the view of where they are located and what relationship they have to the things around them. The hands-on activities in this book reflect the five themes of geography published in the Guidelines for Geographic Education: location, place, human/environment interaction, movement, and regions.

The focus of this book is not for students to simply memorize place names and their locations around the United States, but rather to understand the concepts behind the names and to recognize the relationships between places in the country. The first section of the book contains activities that concentrate on strengthening map skills and understanding the five themes of geography. The second section of the book includes hands-on activities to reinforce a variety of geography concepts centered around the United States. The third section is comprised of charts, graphs, and diagrams that students will encounter on standardized tests. Finally, the appendix contains a variety of rubrics, graphic organizers, the National Geography Standards, and an answer key.

Suggested activities for the United States Map on pages 6-7:
- Make a copy of the map for each student. Have students label each state, draw a star for each capital city, color each state using different-colored pencils, and label the significant bodies of water.
- Make an enlarged copy of the map. Using different-colored markers, color each state. Laminate the map. Place the map and a black, write-on/wipe-away marker at a social studies center. Provide time for each student to label the states correctly. Include a smaller, labeled version of the map at the center for self-checking.
- Make an enlarged copy of the map. Using different-colored markers, color each state. With a black permanent marker, write each state's name. Laminate the map. Cut out each state to make a puzzle. Place the map puzzle in a social studies center. Provide time for each student to assemble the states correctly. Include a smaller, labeled version of the map at the center for self-checking.

Maps: Tools of a Geographer

A **map** is one of the most important tools that a geographer uses. A map is defined as a graphic representation of an area. Maps have been used for many centuries. Explorers used them and updated them as they traveled around the world. Today, maps are used by pilots, bus drivers, truck drivers, and anyone else who needs to locate a place.

The first maps known to exist were made on small pieces of clay. They were drawn in Babylonia. For a long time, people did not know very much about the land beyond their own homes. The early maps only depicted the land on which people traveled. Later, explorers gathered information about bodies of water, continents, and the shapes of islands. As new information was discovered, maps were updated.

Cartographers (map makers) wanted to make an accurate presentation of the information that was gathered. The most accurate way to display this information was to place it on a globe. Since a globe is a round ball similar to the shape of the earth, the continents and oceans could be shown nearly as they actually are. However, there was a problem with the portability of the globe. A globe cannot be folded and put into a pocket like a map can. In addition, globes are limited in the details they can show of a smaller area, such as a city or state.

There are many types of maps:

- **Physical maps** are a common type of map. They show the earth's physical features, such as mountains, oceans, rivers, lakes, deserts, and land elevations. Cities, towns, and borders may also be shown on a physical map.

- **Political maps** show political divisions or boundaries between states, countries, or other governmental units. Some political boundaries follow natural features, such as lakes or rivers. However, most are artificial boundaries that governments have agreed upon. Political maps also show cities and capitals.

- **Population maps** show how people live in an area. Some population maps show population of countries or states. Other population maps show the population of cities or counties.

- **Grid maps** show the specific locations of places based on numbered and lettered horizontal and vertical lines. The grid allows the user to easily locate places on a map. The map is divided into squares by the lines on the grid. Along the top and bottom of the grid, there are letters. On the sides, there are numbers. By using letter-number combinations, locations can be found easily.

Map of the United States

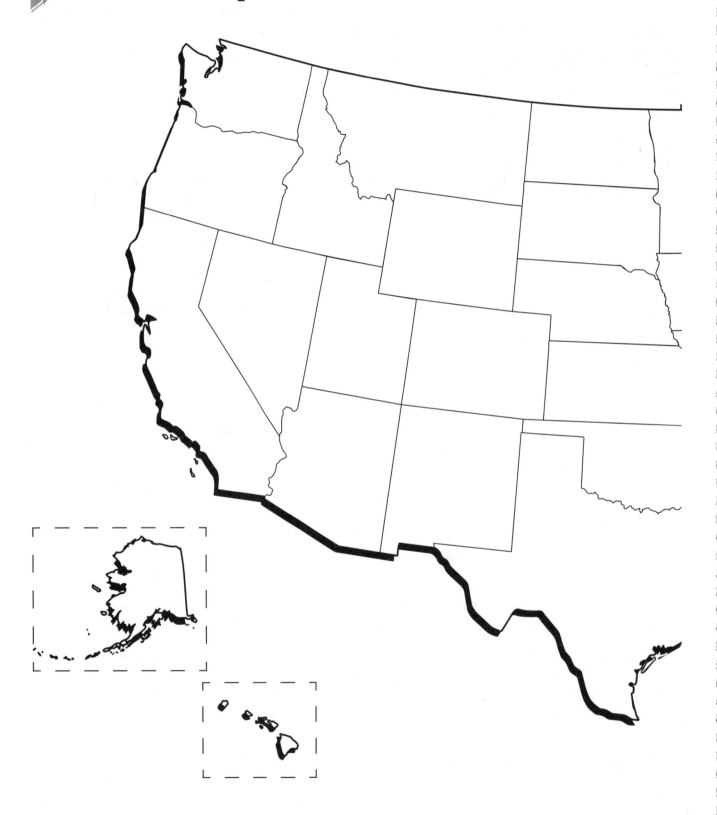

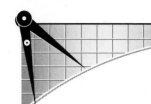

Drawing a Compass Rose

A **compass rose** is a representation of the directions on a map. Sometimes a compass rose shows the four main directions: north, south, east, and west. The letters N, S, E, and W stand for these directions. These are called the **cardinal directions**. Other times, a compass rose shows both the cardinal directions and the **intermediate directions**: northeast, northwest, southeast, and southwest. The letters NE, NW, SE, and SW stand for the four intermediate directions. The intermediate directions are located halfway between the cardinal directions.

The compass rose helps show the directions of things on a map. Not every map shows the north pole, but most maps do have compass roses.

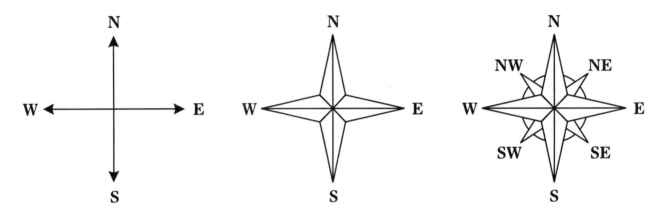

Directions: Choose two of the above compass roses to draw in the boxes provided. In the third box, design a compass rose. Label the cardinal and intermediate directions. Remember that north (N) must be at the top of each compass rose.

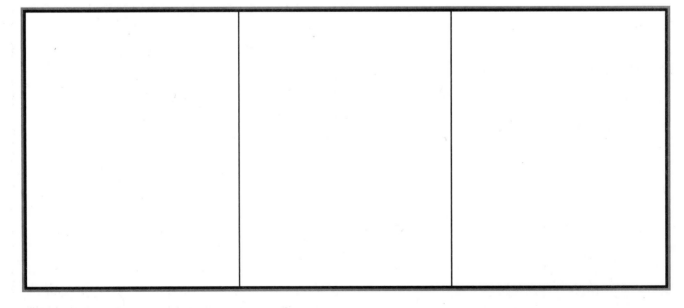

Creating Map Symbols

Maps are drawings of places. **Map symbols** are marks or drawings on the map that represent actual things. The symbols are also shown in a **map key.** A map key explains what each symbol represents.

Directions: The following are some common map symbols. Write the number of each symbol shown beside the correct word below.

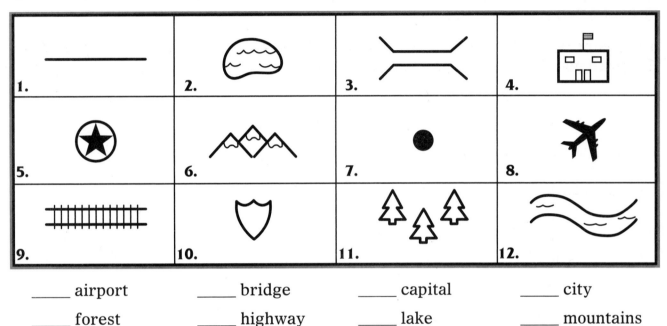

1.	2.	3.	4.
5.	6.	7.	8.
9.	10.	11.	12.

_____ airport   _____ bridge   _____ capital   _____ city

_____ forest   _____ highway   _____ lake   _____ mountains

_____ railroad   _____ river   _____ road   _____ school

Directions: Use the map to answer the following questions.

13. The capital is named _____.

14. The cities are named _____ and _____.

15. Name the river. _____

16. Kelsey is _____ (direction) of Cindy.

17. The mountains are named _____.

18. Name the forest. _____

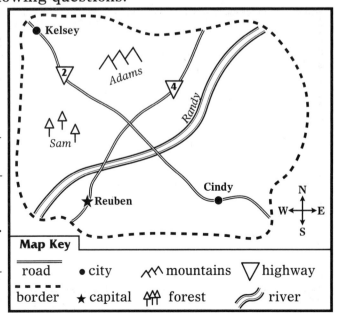

Map Key

road   • city   mountains   highway

border   ★ capital   forest   river

Using a Map Scale

A **map scale** explains how real distances on the earth relate to distances on a map. A map scale shows distances in both miles (mi.) and kilometers (km). Knowing how to read a map scale is necessary to understand actual distance. To measure distances on a map, you will need a ruler. Note the illustrations below.

A   **B**

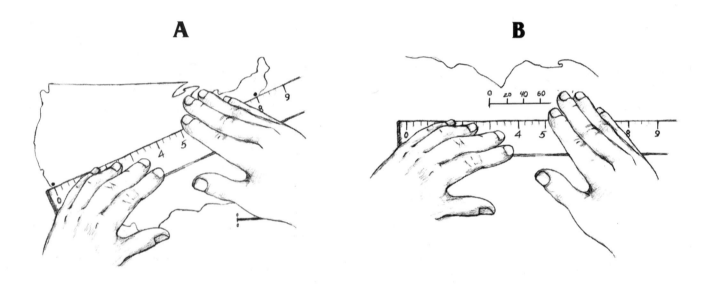

Directions:
Use the map on page 11 to complete this activity.

1. Use a ruler to measure the distance in inches between Rock Springs and Claire. If you measured correctly, the distance is 1".

2. Now, place the ruler on the map scale. How many miles does 1" equal? If you measured correctly, the answer is 100 mi.

3. Next, use the ruler to measure the distance in centimeters between Rock Springs and Claire. If you measured correctly, the distance is 2.5 cm.

4. Place the ruler on the map scale. How many kilometers does 2.5 cm equal? If you measured correctly, the answer is 160 km.

Using a Map Scale

Directions: Review the information on page 10. Use a ruler and this map of the imaginary state of Edison to answer the questions below.

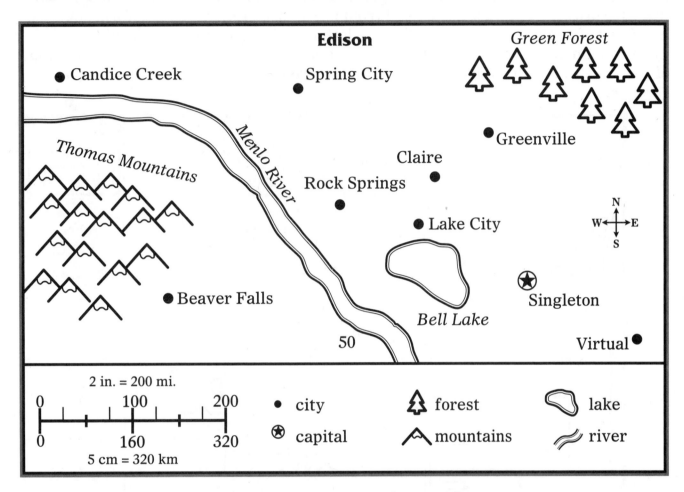

1. How many miles does the scale on the map of Edison show? _____

2. How many miles is it from Claire to Spring City? _____

3. How many kilometers is it from Greenville to Spring City? _____

4. The name of the river is _____.

5. If you traveled from Lake City to Rock Springs and then to Beaver Falls, how many miles would you have traveled? _____

6. How long is the northern border of the state of Edison? _____

7. What is the symbol for mountains? _____

Locating Places on a Grid

When locating a place on a map, sometimes it is necessary to point out exactly where it is. This can be done using a **grid**. A grid is a pattern of lines drawn on a map. Grid lines are drawn from west to east and from north to south. These lines form squares. Each row of squares has a letter. Find the letters written on the left side of the map. Each column of squares is labeled with a number. Locate the numbers across the top of the map. Use both the letter (row) and the number (column) to identify a square.

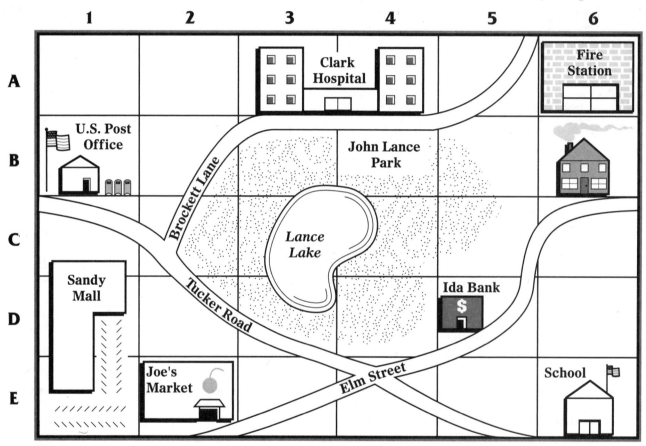

Directions: Use the map to answer the questions.

1. In what square is the post office located? _____

2. Elm Street begins in E-2 and ends in what square? _____

3. In which squares is Clark Hospital? _____

4. What building is in square D-5? _____

5. Which three squares provide the shortest route from the school to the fire station?
_____

Putting It Together: Parts of a Map

In order to use a map correctly, all parts should be used. Most maps have **titles**. A title informs the user about what the map shows. A **map key** or **legend** explains what the symbols on a map mean. Sometimes, the map key contains colors that are used on the map. A **compass rose** shows the directions on a map. The **map scale** is a guide to what distances on the map equal in real life. Most map scales are shown in miles (mi.) and kilometers (km).

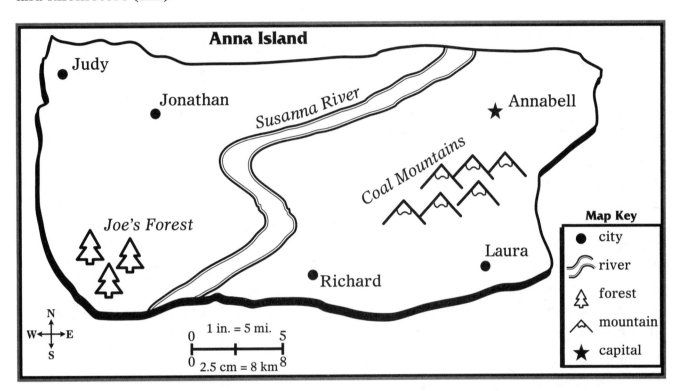

Directions: Study the map above, then answer the following questions.

1. What is the title of the map? _____

2. Where is the explanation for the forest symbol found? _____

3. How many miles is it from the city of Judy to the city of Laura? _____

4. In what direction would you travel to go from Richard to Jonathan? _____

5. In what intermediate direction is the city of Judy located on the map? _____

6. What does the map key say that this symbol 〜 means? _____

7. The capital city of Anna Island is _____.

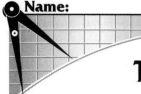
The Five Themes of Geography

To the Teacher: In the Guidelines for Geographic Education, published by the Joint Committee of the National Council for Geographic Education and the Association of American Geographers, five fundamental themes of geography were identified—**location**, **place**, **human/environment interaction**, **movement**, and **regions**. As students and geographers study the earth and its people, these themes help them to organize their information.

Location is the position of places and people on the earth. Location can be described in two ways: **absolute** and **relative**. Absolute location is an exact position based on the grid system of lines of latitude and longitude. Relative location describes a place in relation to what it is near or around.

Place is described using two kinds of features—**physical** and **human**. Physical features include landforms, altitude, climate, soil, and plant and animal life. Human features include population, housing, language, economy, customs, and beliefs.

Human/Environment Interaction describes the ways in which people and their environment interact and the physical characteristics of their surroundings. Human/environment interaction can be positive or negative. When people pollute the environment, cut down trees, farm the land, conserve resources, or recycle materials, they are interacting with their environment.

Movement describes how people, goods, and ideas move from one part of the earth to another. When geographers study movement, they look at transportation, communication, and the cause-and-effect relationships of movement.

Regions are the basic units for the study of geography. Various features are used to classify a place as a region. A region shares the same features, such as climate, land, history, population, or natural resources.

Directions: Write which theme of geography is being asked about in each question.

1. What is the absolute location of New Orleans, Louisiana? _____

2. In which U.S. region is the state of Oregon found? _____

3. What are Georgia's two main crops? _____

4. In what state can you find the most mountains? _____

5. What is the best mode of travel to go from Chicago to Miami? _____

Lines of Latitude

Lines on a globe or map can be used to help find where places are located. Lines that go around the globe from east to west are called lines of **latitude** or **parallels**. These lines of latitude measure distances north and south of the equator. All lines of latitude are measured in degrees (°). The lines north of the equator are labeled N for north, and the lines south of the equator are labeled S for south. One way to remember latitude is to think of a ladder that you would use to go up or down.

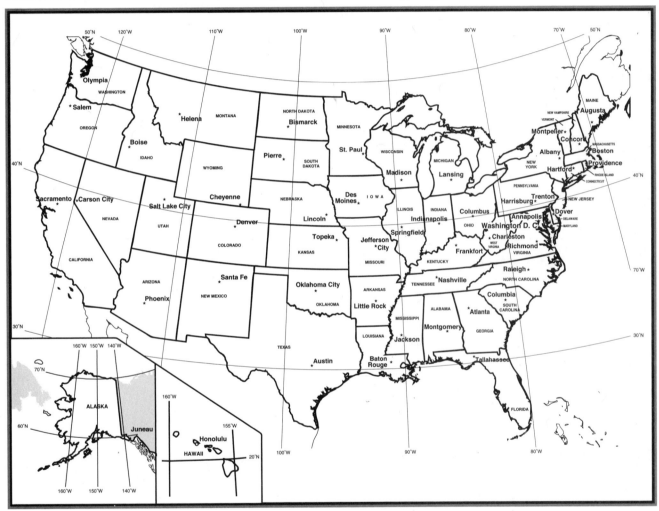

Directions: Use this map of the United States to find the shown line of latitude that is nearest to each of the following capital cities.

1. Austin, Texas _____

2. Dover, Delaware _____

3. Springfield, Illinois _____

4. Denver, Colorado _____

5. Baton Rouge, Louisiana _____

6. Indianapolis, Indiana _____

Lines of Longitude

Lines on a globe or map can be used to help find where places are located. Lines that go around the globe from north to south are called lines of **longitude** or **meridians**. These lines of longitude measure distances east and west of the prime meridian. All lines of longitude are measured in degrees (°). The lines east of the prime meridian are labeled E for east and the lines west of the prime meridian are labeled W for west. One way to remember longitude is to think of the word "long" because these lines measure longways.

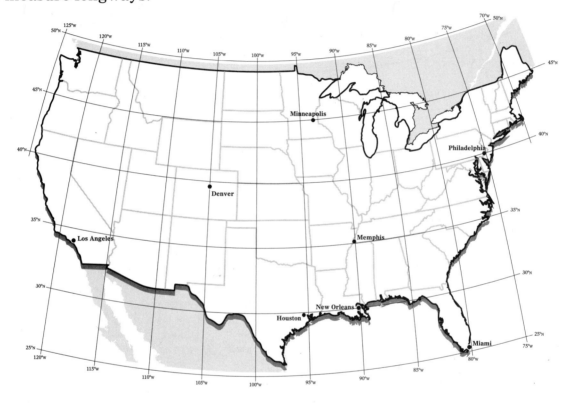

Directions: Use the map of the United States to answer the following questions.

1. Which city is located on 105°W? _____

2. What two cities are found at 90°W? _____

3. Miami is closest to which line of longitude? _____

4. Houston is located near which line of longitude? _____

5. The 75°W line of longitude runs close to _____ .

6. Look carefully to estimate the line of longitude for Minneapolis. _____

Lines of Latitude and Longitude

Directions: Use the U.S. map below to answer the following questions about latitude and longitude. If necessary, review pages 15-16.

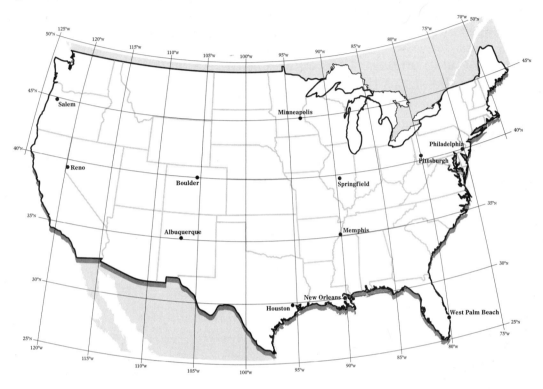

1. What is the approximate latitude and longitude of Pittsburgh?

   A. 45°N, 85°W

   B. 40°N, 75°W

   C. 40°N, 80°W

   D. 40°W, 80°N

2. The city located near 35°N, 107°W is

   A. Boulder.

   B. Albuquerque.

   C. Memphis.

   D. Salem.

3. What is the approximate latitude and longitude of Springfield?

   A. 40°N, 90°W

   B. 27°N, 80°W

   C. 97°W, 45°N

   D. 40°W, 90°N

4. Which two cities are located near 35°N?

   A. Albuquerque and Boulder

   B. Boulder and Springfield

   C. Memphis and Springfield

   D. Albuquerque and Memphis

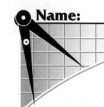

Famous U.S. Rivers

Many of the world's most famous cities began as small towns or settlements along major rivers. This is also true of many cities in the United States. The fresh water from these rivers was used for drinking, irrigating crops, providing food, and transporting people and goods.

Directions: Use the map on page 19 to complete the following chart by either naming each river or listing the states that the river flows through.

Name of River	States the River Flows Through
1. Tennessee	
2.	Louisiana, Mississippi, Arkansas, Iowa, Tennessee, Kentucky, Missouri, Illinois, Wisconsin, Minnesota
3. Red	
4. Arkansas	
5.	Oregon, Washington
6. Ohio	
7. Colorado	
8.	Colorado, Wyoming, Nebraska
9. Missouri	
10. Rio Grande	
11.	Washington, Oregon, Idaho, Wyoming

Activity Extension: Choose one U.S. river listed above to research. Find the important American cities that began along the chosen river.

Famous U.S. Rivers

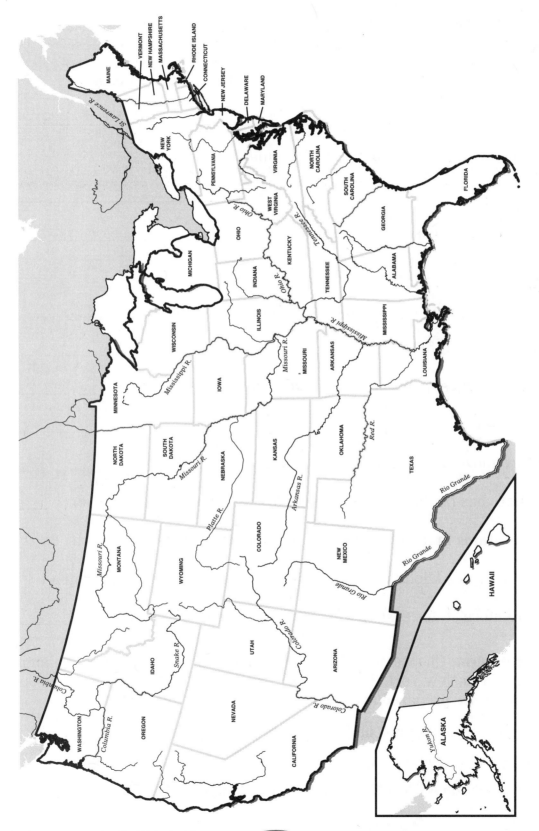

U.S. Deserts and Mountains

Directions: Use the map of U.S. deserts and mountains on page 21 to answer the following questions. If necessary, use an atlas to identify state names.

1. Which mountain range stretches along most of the eastern coast?

   _____

2. Which mountain range is found in Wyoming?

   _____

3. List the four deserts shown on the map. _____

   _____

4. Where is the lowest point in the United States? _____

   In which state is it found? _____

5. What is the highest point in the United States? _____

   In which state is it found? _____

6. Where are most of the U.S. mountain ranges located? _____

7. Which state has the largest percentage of its area covered by desert? _____

8. Circle the states in the following list that do not contain any deserts.

   Oklahoma, Texas, Michigan, Idaho, California, Florida, Maine, Oregon

9. Are there more states east or west of the Rocky Mountains? _____

Activity Extension: Choose one of the following criteria (A, B, or C) to plan a route from California to New York. Use a crayon or colorful pencil to trace the route on the map on page 21. Be prepared to explain why you chose this route.

A. Crossing as few mountains and deserts as possible

B. Crossing as many mountains and deserts as possible

C. Crossing the Mojave Desert, the Rocky Mountains, and the Chihuahuan Desert

U.S. Deserts and Mountains

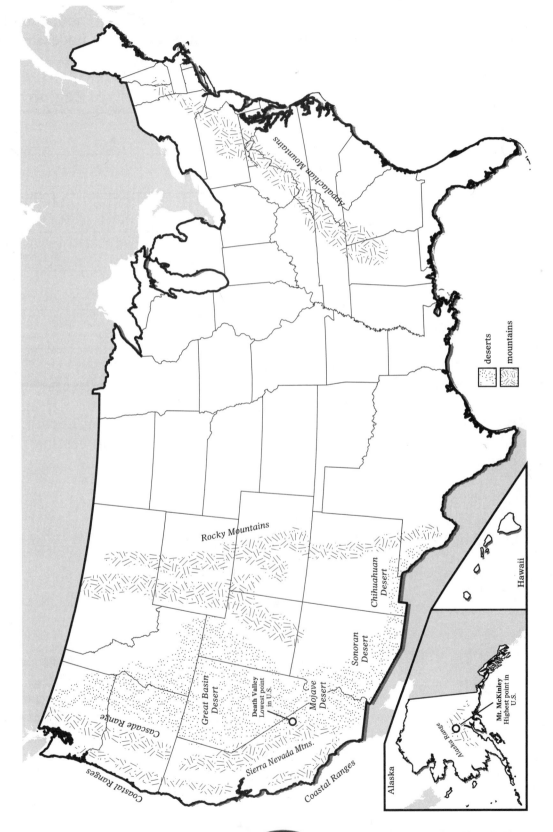

Appalachian Mountains

deserts

mountains

Rocky Mountains

Chihuahuan Desert

Sonoran Desert

Great Basin Desert

Death Valley Lowest point in U.S.

Mojave Desert

Cascade Range

Sierra Nevada Mtns.

Coastal Ranges

Coastal Ranges

Hawaii

Mt. McKinley Highest point in U.S.

Alaska Range

Alaska

Famous U.S. Landmarks

Directions: Identify the famous U.S. landmarks shown on page 23. Then, complete the table below by researching the landmarks' states and regions. If necessary, use pages 30-36 to identify region names.

Number	Name	State(s)	Region
1.	Alamo		
2.	Mount Rushmore		
3.	Gateway Arch		
4.	Statue of Liberty		
5.	Old Faithful		
6.	Golden Gate Bridge		
7.	Grand Canyon		

Activity Extension: Choose one of the landmarks to research further. Locate information about the landmark's history, importance, and other interesting facts. Then, choose one of the following:

A. Create a magazine ad encouraging tourists to visit the landmark.

B. Make a model of the landmark.

C. Design a Web page advertising the landmark's features.

Famous U.S. Landmarks

Directions: Use the information on the chart on page 22 to label each landmark with the number that corresponds with its name.

Creating U.S. Climates

In this activity, you will make a shoe box scene to show the climates found in three U.S. regions.

Materials:

Shoe box
Construction paper
Scissors
Glue
Pen or pencil
Markers

3 index cards
Ruler
Modeling clay
Objects such as stones, twigs, sand, etc.
Drawing paper

Directions:

1. Research the climates of three locations found in three different regions of the United States. (See pages 30-36.)

2. On an index card, write a description of each climate.

3. Turn the shoe box on one of its longest sides.

4. Cut two pieces of construction paper as tall as the opening of the box plus 2" and as wide as the box is deep. Fold back 1" flaps on the top and bottom of the paper.

5. To divide the box into three sections, insert one piece of construction paper into the box opening and glue the flaps to the top and bottom of the box.

6. Repeat Step 5 with the second piece of construction paper.

7. Create a scene showing the climate of each location you researched. Use a variety of objects in your scenes and make them neat and colorful.

8. Label each section with the names of the location and region.

U.S. Natural Resources

The United States is very rich in natural resources. For this reason, it is one of the world's largest producers of manufactured goods. Use the map on page 26 to complete the following activity.

Directions: First, write the name of the natural resource next to each picture. On the lines provided, list the states where each resource can be found. If there are more than five states in a resource category, list only five states.

1.  _____

_____

_____

_____

_____

2.  _____

_____

_____

_____

_____

3.  _____

_____

_____

_____

_____

4. _____

_____

_____

_____

_____

5.  _____

_____

_____

_____

_____

6. _____

_____

_____

_____

_____

7. _____

_____

_____

_____

_____

8.  _____

_____

_____

_____

_____

9.  _____

_____

_____

_____

_____

U.S. Natural Resources

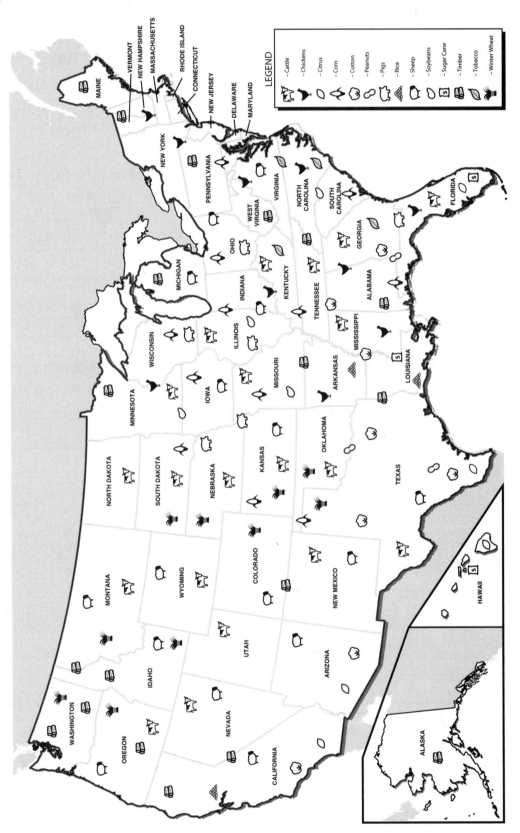

LEGEND

- Cattle
- Chickens
- Citrus
- Corn
- Cotton
- Peanuts
- Pigs
- Rice
- Sheep
- Soybeans
- Sugar Cane
- Timber
- Tobacco
- Winter Wheat

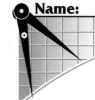
U.S. Cities' Mileage Chart

A **mileage chart** is used to find the distance between two places, which is very helpful when traveling by car. On the mileage chart below, distances are shown between 10 cities in the United States. To use this chart, place a finger on your left hand on a city in the left column and place a finger on your right hand on a city along the top row. Move your fingers together to find the exact mileage. For example, the distance between Denver and New Orleans is 1,279 miles.

	Atlanta	Baltimore	Charleston	Denver	Houston	Los Angeles	Miami	New Orleans	Pittsburgh
Baltimore, MD	669		582	1,700	1,455	2,687	1,080	1,126	251
Charleston, SC	320	582		1,719	1,110	2,573	580	781	650
Denver, CO	1,416	1,700	1,719		1,028	1,023	2,077	1,279	1,460
Houston, TX	802	1,455	1,110	1,028		1,566	1,190	352	1,346
Los Angeles, CA	2,211	2,687	2,573	1,023	1,566		2,752	1,914	2,454
Miami, FL	661	1,080	580	2,077	1,190	2,752		861	1,168
New Orleans, LA	473	1,126	781	1,279	352	1,914	861		1,099
Pittsburgh, PA	683	251	650	1,460	1,346	2,454	1,168	1,099	
Salt Lake City, UT	1,882	2,095	2,185	512	1,488	688	2,543	1,739	1,852

Directions: Use the mileage chart to find the distances between these U.S. cities.

1. Miami to Denver _____   **6.** Baltimore to Pittsburgh _____

2. Salt Lake City to Miami _____   **7.** New Orleans to Atlanta _____

3. Houston to Baltimore _____   **8.** Los Angeles to Atlanta _____

4. Los Angeles to Denver _____   **9.** Denver to Houston _____

5. Charleston to Pittsburgh _____   **10.** Houston to Charleston _____

U.S. Time Zones

The map below shows the various **time zones** in the United States. There are six time zones in the country. They include Eastern, Central, Mountain, Pacific, Alaskan, and Hawaiian. When traveling from the east coast to the west coast, you will go through four time zones. Both Alaska and Hawaii are in their own time zones.

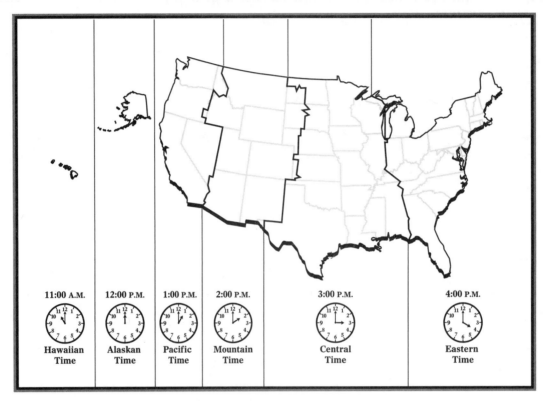

Directions: Use the U.S. time zone map to answer the following questions. If necessary, use an atlas to identify states.

1. In what time zone do you live? _____

2. If it is 3:00 P.M. in Pennsylvania, what time is it in Texas? _____

3. In what time zone is the state of Washington? _____

4. If it is 2:00 P.M. in California, what time is it in Maine? _____

5. In what time zone is the state of Louisiana? _____

6. How many hours difference is there between Missouri and Nevada? _____

7. If it is 5:00 A.M. in Hawaii, what time is it in Oklahoma? _____

U.S. Region Tales

In this activity, geography will be combined with imagination, art, and creative writing skills.

Materials:
Region shape pattern (pages 30-36)
Scissors
Markers
Glue
Other craft materials
Notebook paper
Pen or pencil

Directions:
1. Choose one of the U.S. region shapes from pages 30-36. Enlarge the pattern for one state and cut it out.

2. Look at the state's shape. What does it look like? An animal? A machine?

3. Decorate the state shape using markers and other craft materials.

4. Write a creative story about the origin of the state. Refer to the picture that you created. Relate this story to the U.S. region in which the state is located.

Mountain Region

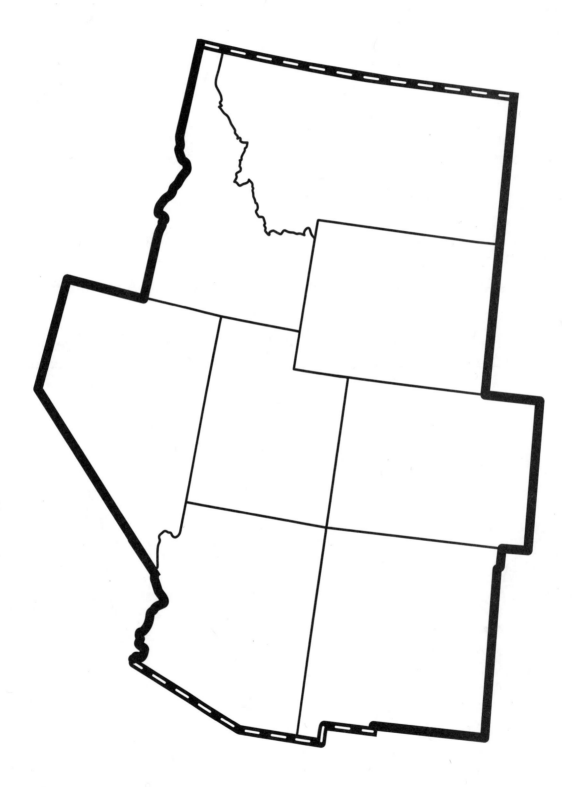

Northern Plains Region

Southern Plains Region

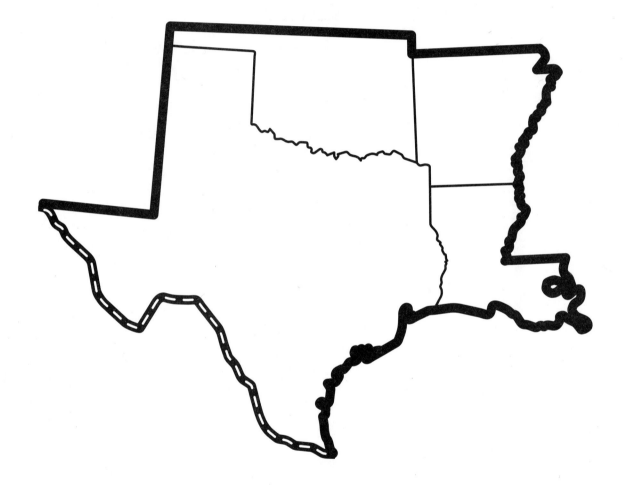

Northeastern Region

Southeastern Region

Midwest Region

Pacific Region

Introduction to Hands-On Activities

One objective of the hands-on geography activities section in this book is to offer fun and involving activities to generate students' interest in geography. Another objective is to reinforce and enhance students' understanding and use of geography tools, such as maps. And lastly, these activities are designed to strengthen students' research and analytical skills. (For each activity that requires research, provide students with reference materials along with the materials listed for the activity.) By completing these activities, students will increase their knowledge of both physical and cultural geography.

Having a solid foundation in geography will provide students with invaluable resources that they will use for the rest of their lives. In the future, students will use their knowledge of geography to select places to live, work, and vacation. As a teacher, you can teach students geographical information they will need to compete and cooperate in a global society.

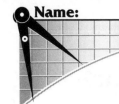

An "Egg-ceptional" World

For this activity, you will make a model showing the main features of a globe.

Materials:
Globe or world map
Light-colored plastic egg
Fine-tipped, black permanent marker
Colorful permanent markers

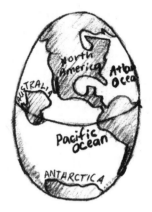

Directions:

1. Locate the seven continents of the world on a globe or world map. Using the globe or map as a guide, draw the shapes of the continents on the plastic egg with a fine-tipped, black permanent marker. The equator is represented by the place where the egg halves snap together.

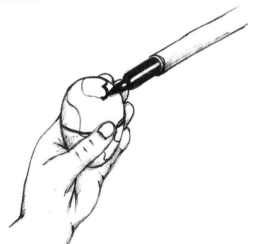

2. When the continents have been drawn, carefully fill in the continents with colorful permanent markers.

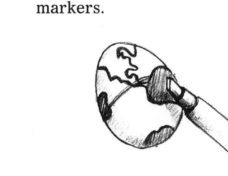

3. With a fine-tipped, black permanent marker, label the continents and oceans.

My Own World

The following activity provides a way to create a convenient-sized and lightweight globe to hang anywhere.

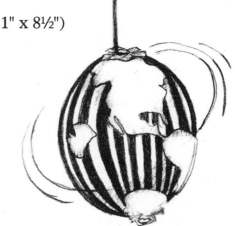

Materials:

12 strips of blue construction paper (approximately 1" x 8½")
2 brass fasteners
Hole punch
Copy of a blank world map (8" x 11½")
Markers or colorful pencils
Scissors
Glue
String or yarn

Directions:

1. Punch a hole in the top and bottom of each strip of blue construction paper.

4. On a copy of a blank world map, label, color, and cut out each continent.

2. Attach the paper strips together with brass fasteners at the top and bottom.

5. Glue the continents onto the paper sphere in the correct locations. When the glue has dried, attach a string or piece of yarn to the top fastener so that the globe may be hung.

3. Spread out the paper strips to make a sphere.

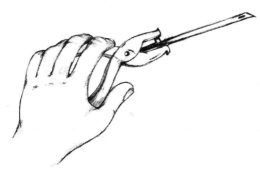

Compass Rose Creation

This project involves creating a compass rose containing both cardinal and intermediate directions.

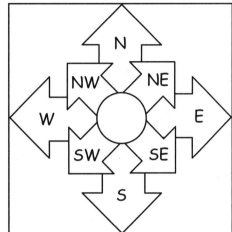

Materials:
Construction paper (various colors)
Glue
Scissors
Large arrow pattern (page 41)
Small arrow pattern (page 41)
Circle pattern (page 41)
Pencil

Directions:

1. Use the large arrow pattern to trace four arrows on colorful construction paper.

2. Carefully cut out the four arrows.

3. Use the small arrow pattern to trace four arrows on colorful construction paper. (Select a different color than the one used for the large arrows.)

4. Carefully cut out the four smaller arrows.

5. Glue the larger arrows to the center of a large piece of construction paper so that they point in four different directions.

6. Label the four cardinal directions: N, S, E, and W.

7. Glue the four smaller arrows to the same piece of construction paper so that they point in the four intermediate directions.

8. Label the four intermediate directions: NE, NW, SE, and SW.

9. Use the circle pattern to trace a circle on white construction paper.

10. Carefully cut out the circle and glue it to cover where the arrows come together.

To the Teacher: As an extension, create a large version of the compass rose and mount it to the ceiling. Have students go to various locations in the classroom. Next, ask a student to move and tell in which direction he is going. Or, play an "I Spy" game in which students locate items you have hidden in your classroom. Use directional words to help students find the items.

Arrow and Circle Patterns

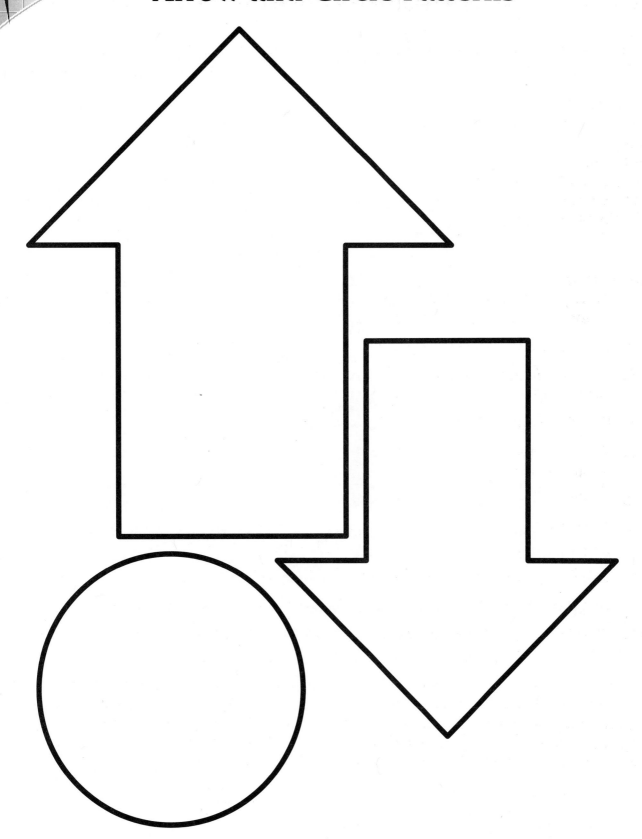

User-Friendly Coordinate Map

This map will show where latitude and longitude coordinates cross.

Materials:
Copy of a world map (with latitude and longitude lines in a Mercator projection)
Scissors
Glue
Blank file folder with tab cut off
2 colors of yarn

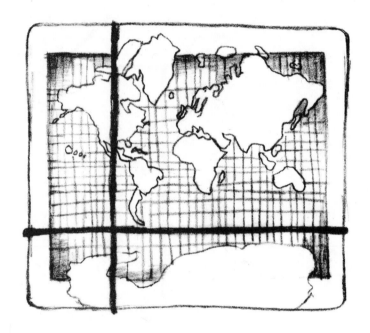

Directions:
1. Have an adult glue a copy of a world map to a blank file folder and laminate for durability.

2. Cut one piece of yarn so that it will wrap horizontally around the folder.

3. Wrap the yarn around the folder horizontally and tie. The yarn should be loose enough to slide from top to bottom.

4. Cut a piece of different-colored yarn so that it will wrap vertically around the folder.

5. Wrap the yarn around the folder vertically and tie. The yarn should be loose enough to slide from side to side.

6. As various locations are given by latitude and longitude, find them by sliding the yarn to locate the line of latitude and then the line of longitude. The location of the place given is where the two pieces of yarn intersect.

Fun with Flip Books

During the study of the five themes of geography, use a flip book to help reinforce the concepts.

Materials:
3 colorful paper strips (4¼" x 11")
Markers or colorful pencils
Magazines
Stapler
Scissors
Glue

Directions*:
1. Line up the three pieces of paper so that the bottom of each sheet extends ¾" beyond the sheet above it.

2. While holding the three pieces of paper together, fold them so that the top of the first sheet is ¾" from the bottom of the first sheet.

3. Staple the top of the flip book.

4. Label the top flap (the cover) "The Five Themes of Geography."

5. On the next five flaps, label each with one of the themes: Location, Place, Human/Environment Interaction, Movement, and Regions.

6. Then, write the definition of each theme underneath the previous flap.

7. Draw or use pictures cut from magazines to illustrate each theme.

The Five Themes of Geography
Location
Place
Human/Environment Interaction
Movement
Regions

*See step-by-step diagrams on page 44.

Fun with Flip Books

Book Diagrams

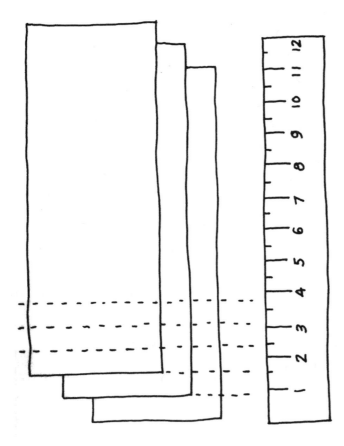

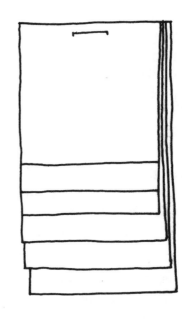

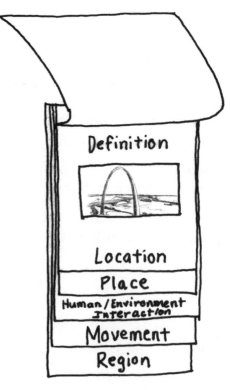

The Five
Themes
of
Geography

| Location |
| Place |
| Human/Environment Interaction |
| Movement |
| Region |

Definition

| Location |
| Place |
| Human/Environment Interaction |
| Movement |
| Region |

A "Handy" Landform Reference

This activity provides a convenient resource to introduce landform terms.

Materials:

White paper   Poster board
Pencil   Markers or colorful pencils
Glue   Scissors

Directions:

1. Trace either open hand on a piece of white paper.

2. Cut out the hand outline.

3. Glue the hand outline to a piece of colorful poster board.

4. Create an island map using the hand outline.

5. Name the hand island and label it.

6. Choose three of the following water features to draw on the map: river, lake, ocean, harbor, sea, or waterfall.

7. Next, name and label the three water features. (If needed, use an atlas, geography book, or other resource.)

8. Choose four of the following land features to draw on the island: mountain, hill, beach, desert, peninsula, plain, valley, or volcano. Next, name and label the four land features. (If needed, use an atlas, geography book, or other resource.)

9. Create a key and a compass rose for the island map.

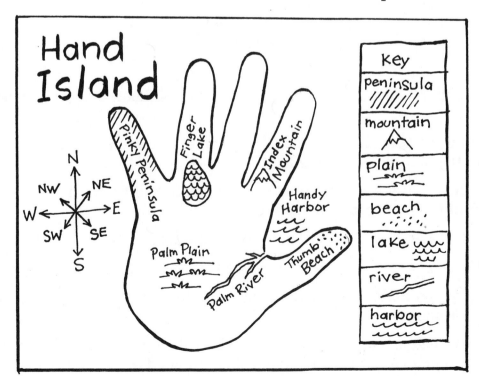

Build-Your-Own Landforms

This activity will get the class involved in learning about and recognizing different landforms (and may be a little messy).

Materials:

5 lbs. salt
2 cups water
1 lb. cornstarch
2 cups water
Cardboard
Craft paint (earth tones, blues, and greens)

Jars or plastic containers with lids
Large pan
Mixing bowl
Craft paintbrushes
Small, adhesive labels
Toothpicks

Directions:

1. Mix cornstarch with 2 cups of water and set aside.

2. Let an adult mix salt and 2 cups of water in a pan and heat it on a stove at medium temperature.

3. With adult supervision, stir until the mixture is well heated, approximately five minutes.

4. Have an adult remove the pan from the heat, add the cornstarch and water mixture to the pan, and stir quickly.

5. If the mixture does not thicken, have an adult return it to the stove on low heat and stir until thick. A soft, pliable clay should form.

6. Let an adult place the clay in jars or plastic containers with lids until cool.

7. After cooling for at least one hour, remove the clay and place it on cardboard.

8. Mold the clay to create various landforms, such as a mountain, hill, valley, plain, peninsula, or volcano.

9. Insert a toothpick in each landform, then allow the clay to dry. Paint each landform and label it with an adhesive label attached to the toothpick.

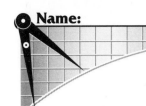

Edible Map

To the Teacher: Before completing any food activity, ask families' permission and inquire about students' food allergies and religious or other food preferences.

To the Student: When studying a particular state, here is a fun way to make a map that you and your classmates can really sink your teeth into. This is best done as a whole class activity with the teacher or another adult as the guide.

Materials:
Prepared or homemade cookie dough
Aluminum foil
Cookie sheet
Table knife
Atlas
Icing (blue, green, and yellow)
Chocolate chips
Candy-covered chocolates and other assorted candy

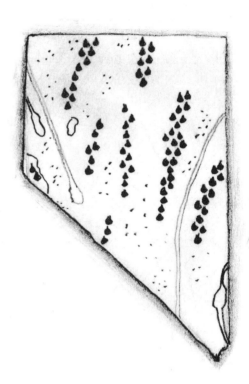

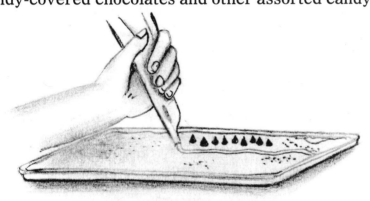

Directions:
1. Following the cookie dough recipe, have an adult bake one large, thick cookie on a cookie sheet. Hint: line the cookie sheet with foil for easy cookie removal.

2. While the cookie is still warm, have an adult cut it into the shape of the desired state.

3. Use an atlas as a guide to create the land and water features of the state.

4. Use blue icing for bodies of water, green icing for grassland, and yellow icing for deserts or other distinct land features.

5. Use chocolate chips to represent mountains.

6. Use candy to represent cities and other land and water features.

7. Create a key for the edible map.

8. Then, eat and enjoy the class creation.

A "State-ly" Book

At the end of a unit of study on a state, complete this bookmaking activity. It works as an individual or group activity. Follow the instructions below to create the book. See page 49 for directions to assemble the book.

Materials: white paper, pen, pictures of the state, glue, scissors

Directions:

1. **Cover:** On white paper, design a cover for the book that will represent the state. Make a collage of pictures cut from travel magazines or brochures, and the Internet.

2. **Table of Contents:** Make a table of contents listing each page that will be included in the book. Number each page as you create it and fill in the page numbers in the table of contents after the pages are complete.

3. **Physical Map:** Using a textbook, atlas, encyclopedia, or other resources, draw a physical map of the state. Include the major physical features. Also include a key and a compass rose.

4. **Political Map:** Using a textbook, atlas, encyclopedia, or other resources, draw a political map of the state. Include the major cities and bordering states, as well as a key and a compass rose.

5. **Key Facts:** Include a list of 20 important facts about the state. Incorporate common key facts, such as the state's symbols, as well as the most interesting or fun facts available.

6. **Biographical Sketches:** Research three important people from the state. Write a paragraph telling about each person and her contributions.

7. **Government:** Use an almanac, the Internet, or other resources to find information about the current leaders and other important governmental officials of the state.

8. **Economy:** Use an almanac, the Internet, or other resources to describe the ways that the people in this state earn money. Include information about farming, tourism, manufacturing, and other related information.

9. **Geography:** Research and write a paragraph describing the main geographical regions of the state.

10. **Travel Guide:** Describe the major points of interest in this state. Include pictures, descriptions, and locations.

11. **Resources:** In alphabetical order, according to the authors' last names, list the resources used in creating this book.

A "State-ly" Book

Materials:

Book pages
White paper
Stapler
Lightweight cardboard
Ruler

Transparent tape
Contact paper, wrapping paper, or fabric
Glue
Scissors
Cover page collage

Directions:

1. Set aside the cover page collage. Then, stack all of the pages neatly in order.

2. Next, put a sheet of white paper on the top and bottom of the stack.

3. Staple the pages together on the left side about ½" from the edge.

4. Cut two pieces of lightweight cardboard. Each piece should be about 1" larger than the book pages.

5. Place the two pieces of cardboard next to each other, leaving about ½" between them. Tape them together.

6. Place the covering material facedown on a work surface. Then, place the cardboard on top of the covering material. Glue the covering material to the cardboard, leaving a 1" border on all sides.

7. Fold the edges of covering material over the cardboard and glue into place.

8. On the inside of the cardboard covers, glue the blank pages of the book. Finally, glue the cover collage to the outside of the book. Let the book dry before allowing others to read it.

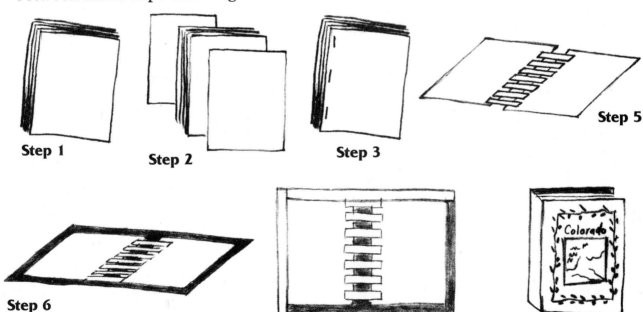

Step 1   Step 2   Step 3   Step 5

Step 6   Step 7   Step 8

Sing a Region Song

Many songs have been written about the United States. In some of these songs, there are references to the different U.S. regions. (See pages 30-36.) One such example is the song, "This Land Is Your Land." Read the song's lyrics below.

This Land Is Your Land

by Woody Guthrie

This land is your land,
This land is my land
From California to the New York island
From the redwood forest
To the Gulf Stream waters;
This land was made for you and me.

As I was walking that ribbon of highway,
I saw above me that endless skyway.
I saw below me that golden valley,
This land was made for you and me.

I've roamed and rambled
And I followed my footsteps
To the sparkling sands of her diamond deserts,
And all around me a voice was sounding,
"This land was made for you and me."

When the sun comes shining
And I was strolling
And the wheat fields waving
And the dust clouds rolling,
As the fog was lifting a voice was chanting,
"This land was made for you and me."

Directions:

1. List words or phrases from the song that describe your region of the country.

_____

_____

_____

_____

2. Make a list of other physical features of your region. Refer to a textbook, encyclopedia, or other resources as needed.

_____

_____

_____

_____

3. On a separate sheet of paper, write a region song using some of the features listed above.

Banner Work

In this activity, state banners will be designed to feature each state's significant symbols, song, flag, or motto.

Materials:
12" x 18" pieces of felt in assorted colors
30" piece of yarn
12" wooden dowel
Scissors
Magazines
Glue
Permanent markers
Decorative trim

Directions:
1. Place the dowel on one of the 12" sides of felt about 1" from the edge.

2. Center the dowel and lay the yarn beside the dowel.

3. Glue along the edge of the felt and fold it over to cover the dowel and the yarn. Hold the felt in place and allow the glue to dry.

4. Cut the corners off the bottom of the felt so that it comes to a point.

5. Choose a state and cut out pictures of its symbols (seal, bird, tree, flower, and flag) from magazines or print them from the Internet. Attach the pictures to different colors of felt. Glue the pictures to the banner and allow it to dry.

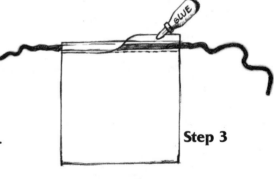

Step 3

6. Use a permanent marker to print the name of the state on the banner.

7. Finish the banner's design by gluing decorative trim around the borders.

8. Tie a bow with the ends of the yarn and display.

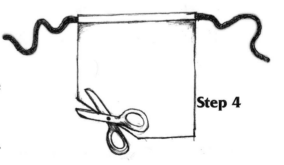

Step 4

A License to Design

After studying a state, the information can be used to design an original state license plate.

Materials:
8½" x 11" white paper
6" x 12" white poster board
Markers
Pictures of state symbols
Scissors
Glue

Directions:

1. Use a sheet of white paper to plan the license plate. Decide which colors to use for the letters, numbers, and background.

2. Lightly decorate a 6" x 12" piece of poster board to create the background of the license plate.

3. Print the name of the state at the top of the license plate.

4. Print the state's nickname or motto at the bottom.

5. In the middle of the license plate, write your initials, a hyphen, and the year you were born to represent the license plate number.

6. Draw or cut out a picture that represents the state, such as the state tree, flower, bird, or other symbol. Glue the picture to the license plate.

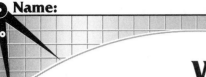
Wish You Were Here

Turn a simple, unlined index card into a colorful, interesting state postcard.

Materials:

3" x 5" unlined index card
Fine-tipped markers
Pen

Directions:

1. Choose a state.

2. On one side of the index card, draw a colorful picture of a famous landmark or tourist attraction found in the state.

3. On the other side, write a short note to a friend or relative describing this famous location.

4. Design a stamp representing that state.

Activity Extension: When the postcards are complete, use pushpins to display them around a U.S. map that has been posted on a bulletin board. Stretch a piece of yarn from each postcard to its corresponding state on the map.

A Mobile for Alabama

After researching a state, use the facts to create a mobile featuring the interesting information that you found.

Materials:

Yarn or string   Card stock or poster board
Glue   Markers or colorful pencils
Scissors   Hole punch
Wire coat hanger

Directions:

1. Based on state research, draw and cut out 10 shapes that relate to the state (important people, places, and/or things that help describe the state).

2. Write a description or facts on the back of each shape.

3. Punch a hole in the top of each shape. Then, tie a piece of yarn through each hole.

4. Attach the yarn to a coat hanger to make the mobile.

5. Make a colorful label to attach to the top of the mobile to identify the state.

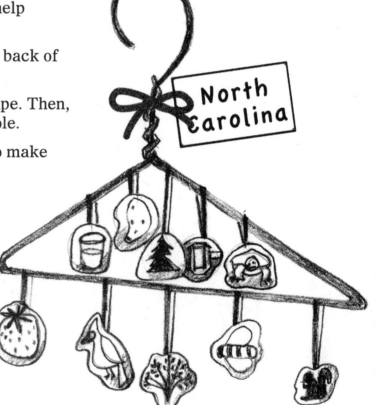

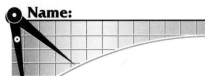

U.S.A. Cooking Day

To the Teacher: Before completing any food activity, ask families' permission and inquire about students' food allergies and religious or other food preferences.

To the Student: Complete this activity after studying the various states. Everyone can prepare and bring a dish representing one of the United States.

Materials:
4" x 6" index card   9" x 12" white poster board
Construction paper   Markers or colorful pencils

Directions:

1. Research the state to find the main agricultural products grown there.

2. Find a recipe that uses one or more of the state's agricultural products. Write the recipe on an index card.

3. On a piece of construction paper, create a place mat that represents the state. Make the place mat colorful and interesting.

4. Design a menu featuring the chosen recipe, as well as other dishes originating from the state. Fold the poster board in half longways to make a menu. On the outside, write a restaurant name that is catchy and refers to the state. On the inside, print several menu items with brief descriptions and suggested prices.

5. On the designated day, bring the menu, place mat, recipe, and dish to class.

Activity Extension: When the recipe cards are complete, use pushpins to display them around a U.S. map that has been posted on a bulletin board. Stretch a piece of yarn from each recipe card to its corresponding state on the map.

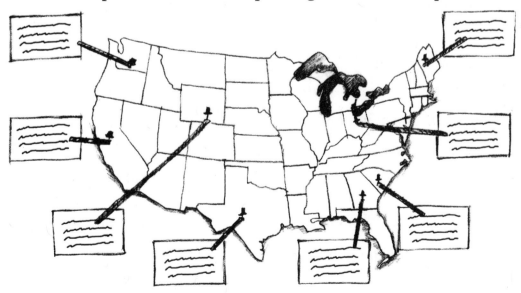

"Geo-Fact-o-Gon"

When first learning about a state or completing a state unit, this is a fun activity, and it makes a nice hanging display.

Materials:
Enlarged copy of the "Geo-Fact-o-Gon" pattern (page 57)
Markers or colorful pencils
String or yarn
Glue
Scissors

Directions:
1. Cut around the outside edge of the pattern.

2. Turn the pattern to the side without lines and label the squares with the following categories: Places of Interest, Climate, Economy, Government, Landforms, and People. Then, write information about each category in the correct square.

3. Write the state's name and region on one of the hexagons. Draw the state's flag on the other hexagon.

4. Lightly color the sections with different colors from the state's flag.

5. Turn the pattern to the side with lines and place a piece of string or yarn where it is indicated on the pattern.

6. Fold the tabs and the square sections of the pattern upward along the dashed lines.

7. Glue the tabs to the edges of the hexagon and one square.

8. Bring the string's ends together and tie them. Display the "Geo-Fact-o-Gon" by hanging it in the classroom for others to learn about the state.

Suggested information for the "Geo-Fact-o-Gon":

- **Places of Interest**—state parks, historical sites, amusement parks

- **Climate**—rainfall, highest and lowest temperatures

- **Economy**—crops, minerals, major businesses, industries

- **Government**—capital, head of state government, number of counties or parishes, date of statehood

- **Landforms**—area, mountains, rivers, deserts, other major landforms

- **People**—first inhabitants, population, food, famous people

"Geo-Fact-o-Gon" Pattern

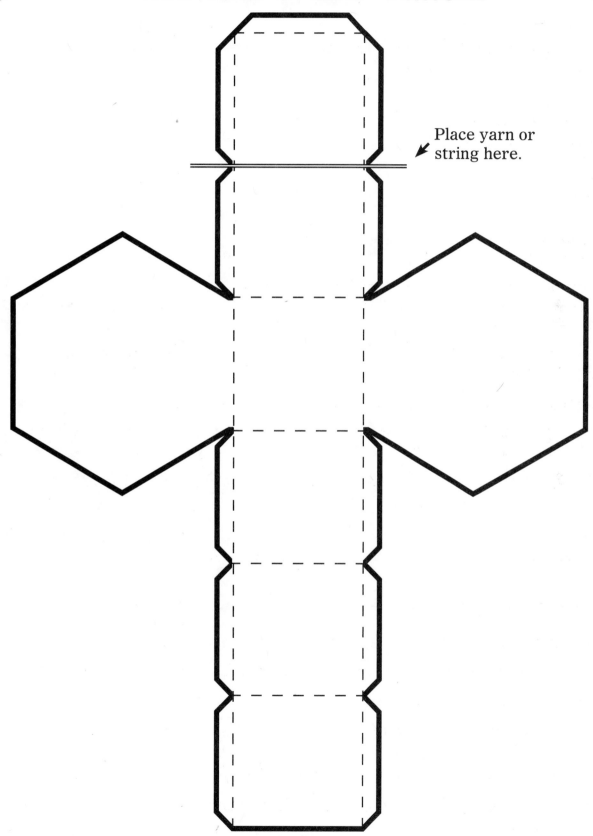

Place yarn or string here.

Quilt of States

This activity involves everyone's creative effort and many fabric squares.

Materials:
Fabric markers
6½" x 6½" light-colored or white squares of fabric
Colorful piece of broadcloth (4½" wider and 4½" taller than assembled fabric squares)
Sewing machine and supplies
Pencil

Directions:
1. Select a state. Then, choose a symbol, landmark, physical feature, or flag that represents that state.

2. Use a pencil to sketch the picture on a fabric square. Then, use fabric markers to trace over and color the picture. Label the square with the state's name.

3. Have an adult collect the completed fabric squares, sew them together, and back the attached fabric squares with colorful broadcloth, leaving a 1" border around the edge.

4. Display the finished quilt.

Bag-a-State

This activity utilizes simple lunch bags to create unique state reports.

Materials:
Paper lunch bag
Markers or colorful pencils
Glue
Scissors
Construction paper
Fabric scraps
Wooden craft sticks
Index cards

Directions:
1. Research a state. Gather the following information:
   A. Capital city
   B. Capital city's latitude and longitude
   C. Governor
   D. Crops
   E. Minerals
   F. Climate(s)
   G. Vegetation
   H. Famous landmarks
   I. Main landforms
   J. Main bodies of water
   K. Flag
   L. Shape of the state
   M. First inhabitants
   N. Famous people

2. Use the information to decorate the outside of the bag.

3. Complete the following and place them inside the bag:
   A. On index cards, list five facts about the state that are not shown on the outside of the bag.
   B. Use glue, fabric scraps, markers, and wooden craft sticks to make puppets of famous people from the state.
   C. Gather three small items that represent the state, such as toys or coins.
   D. Draw or find pictures of three famous landmarks or physical features.

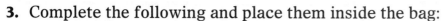

Challenging State Trivia

Directions: After studying the 50 states, review with this trivia game. The trivia cards (pages 60-61) may be enlarged, copied, cut out, and glued to colorful index cards.

1. This state became the site of the first powered airplane flight made by two brothers.	**9.** One of this state's nicknames is the "Cotton State." It was the home of Helen Keller and Governor George Wallace.	**17.** Located in the Great Plains region, Lewis and Clark explored this "Cornhuskers" state in 1804.
2. During the Revolutionary War, this state's Green Mountain Boys, led by Ethan Allen, fought against the British.	**10.** The "Hawkeye State" is a major agricultural state producing corn, hogs, and soybeans.	**18.** Among the major cities in this state are Hartford, Bridgeport, and New Haven.
3. When people think of this state, they might picture potatoes. It grows more potatoes than any other state.	**11.** This state has many natural wonders—among them is the first national park, Yellowstone, home to the famous "Old Faithful."	**19.** Home to the Kennedy Space Center, Disney World, Busch Gardens, and the Everglades, this is the "Sunshine State."
4. Mark Twain, one of this state's most famous citizens, wrote about his experiences along the Mississippi River.	**12.** "The Land of Enchantment," as this state is called, became the 47th state. It is famous for its link to "Billy the Kid."	**20.** The capital city of Salt Lake City is located near the Great Salt Lake. Brigham Young helped make this state famous.
5. The most famous tourist attraction in this state is the giant sculpture carved into a mountainside.	**13.** Jimmy Carter, Hank Aaron, Ted Turner, and Martin Luther King, Jr., have all called this state home.	**21.** Oil wells, cattle, the Houston Space Center, and the Alamo can all be found in this large state.
6. On December 7, 1941, the Japanese attacked a U.S. Naval base, Pearl Harbor, located in this state.	**14.** In 1848, gold was discovered in this state at Sutter's Mill. Three presidents also have connections to this state.	**22.** Often called the "Land of the Midnight Sun," this state is the largest U.S. state and is known for its oil.
7. The smallest state contains 36 islands. The largest of these is called "Aquidneck."	**15.** The "Hoosier State" holds an annual car race known as the Indianapolis 500 on Memorial Day weekend each year.	**23.** This state's name means "great lake" and is made of two large peninsulas.
8. With the capital of Augusta, this is the only state that shares its border with only one other state.	**16.** Football great Barry Sanders and aviator Amelia Earhart both called the "Sunflower State" home.	**24.** The "Silver State" can also boast that it is the largest gold-producing state in the nation.

Challenging State Trivia

25. The Grand Coulee Dam, the nation's largest producer of hydroelectric power, is located in this state.

26. This state, which contains Bismarck, Fargo, and Grand Rapids, became the 39th state.

27. Known as the "Land of Lincoln," this state is considered to be the leading industrial state today.

28. Famous for its dairy products, this state is also the nation's leading producer of ginseng, beets, peas, and snap beans.

29. The first major industry in this state began in 1802, when the famous Du Pont family began manufacturing gun powder.

30. Over half of the Civil War battles were fought on the soil of this state, which is called "Old Dominion."

31. Rocky Mountain National Park, Mesa Verde National Park, and Dinosaur National Monument are famous sites in this state.

32. Many legendary people of the Wild West, such as Geronimo, Wyatt Earp, and Doc Holliday, ventured into this state.

33. The United States Naval Academy was founded on October 10, 1845 in this state's capital, Annapolis.

34. Music has always been an important part of this state's heritage, which includes bluegrass and gospel.

35. With low marsh and bayou land, this state is divided into "parishes" rather than counties.

36. The home of Welch's® and Wal-Mart®, this state also has natural hot springs.

37. Myrtle Beach and Hilton Head Island are sites of beaches, resorts, and golf courses in this state.

38. Glacier National Park and Bighorn Canyon are famous tourist attractions in this state.

39. Known as the "Keystone State," it is the chocolate capital of the nation.

40. George Washington gave this state its nickname "The Empire State," and five U.S. presidents have associations with this state.

41. The birthplace of Elvis Presley, B. B. King, and Tammy Wynette, this state is called "The Magnolia State."

42. This state's motto "Live Free or Die" was written by Revolutionary General John Stark.

43. Four former presidents, John Kennedy, George Bush, John Adams, and John Quincy Adams, all called this state their home.

44. Called the "Bluegrass State," this state holds much of the nation's gold supply at Fort Knox.

45. Once known for its coal mines, today it also relies on clay, petroleum, natural gas, gravel, and salt.

46. Called "The Beaver State," it contains 110 recreational areas and has over 200 state parks.

47. This state became a leading producer of ships and ammunition during the first half of the 20th century.

48. "Land of a Thousand Lakes" is one of the many nicknames of this state, which contains over 15,000 lakes.

49. This state has many natural resources. Called "The Sooner State," it has large deposits of natural gas and coal.

50. This state is home to the first professional baseball team, the Cincinnati Reds.

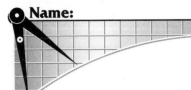
Find the Region Game

This game provides a fun way to culminate the study of U.S. regions.

Teacher Directions:

1. Write each U.S. location listed below on an index card.

2. Divide the class into two teams.

3. Choose a card and read the place listed to the class.

4. Have a player from the first team tell the U.S. region where this place is located. If he is correct, have the team send one player to a posted U.S. map to pinpoint the location with a pushpin. If the team correctly answers both parts of the question, give them the card. If they answer incorrectly, allow the other team to try to identify the region and where the place is located on the map.

5. The team holding the most cards at the end of the game wins.

U.S. Locations

1. United States Space and Rocket Center
2. Mt. McKinley
3. Grand Canyon
4. Crater of Diamonds State Park
5. Yosemite National Park
6. Dinosaur National Park
7. Disney World
8. Martin Luther King, Jr., Historic Site
9. Pearl Harbor
10. Sears Tower
11. Mammoth Cave
12. Camp David
13. Plymouth Rock
14. Gateway Arch
15. Glacier National Park
16. Hoover Dam
17. Atlantic City
18. Statue of Liberty
19. Kitty Hawk
20. Bismarck
21. Liberty Bell
22. Providence
23. Fort Sumter
24. Mount Rushmore
25. Grand Ole Opry
26. Rocky Mountains
27. Great Salt Lake
28. Williamsburg
29. Mount Rainier
30. Allegheny Mountains
31. Yellowstone National Park
32. Niagara Falls
33. Gettysburg
34. Mount St. Helens
35. Appalachian Mountains
36. Alamo
37. Old Faithful
38. Everglades
39. Hilton Head
40. Lake Erie

Traveling the U.S. Regions

In this activity, an imaginary trip around the United States will require the use and knowledge of a mileage chart and U.S. regions.

Directions: Imagine taking a trip around the United States. Fill in the chart below to record your travels. During the trip, you must visit each of the seven U.S. regions. (See pages 30-36.) Begin the trip by filling in the name of your hometown and your region in the spaces labeled City 1. Then, choose one city in each remaining region to complete the first column and top row of the chart. Use the mileage chart in a U.S. road atlas to find the number of miles between the cities listed on your chart. Record the numbers in the boxes where the cities in the top row and first column intersect. List the number of miles between the same city as zero.

	City 1: Region:	City 2: Region:	City 3: Region:	City 4: Region:	City 5: Region:	City 6: Region:	City 7: Region:
City 1: Region:							
City 2: Region:							
City 3: Region:							
City 4: Region:							
City 5: Region:							
City 6: Region:							
City 7: Region:							

Bingo in the Pacific Region

To the Teacher: Pages 64-65 use the classic bingo rules to review facts about two of the seven U.S. regions. You may create additional bingo games for the remaining regions.

Teacher Directions:

1. For each player, copy the boxes below on colorful paper. To create each game board, cut apart the boxes, reassemble them into five by five grids in random order, and glue them to card stock. Laminate the game boards for durability.

2. Let each player use a write-on/wipe-away marker to mark her answers as the clues are called. Let the bingo caller use a write-on/wipe-away marker to mark all clues as they are called.

3. Have the caller give oral clues (for example, "the state flower of Washington," or "the nickname of Hawaii") for the answers written on the cards.

4. The winner is the first player to correctly cover five boxes in any direction.

Juneau	**Golden State**	**Hibiscus**		**Willow Goldfinch**
Willow Ptarmigan		**Sacramento**	**Aloha State**	
Nene	**Rhododendron**	**Beaver State**	**"The Union"**	**Olympia**
"Eureka! I have found it!"	**Golden Poppy**		**Honolulu**	**"Last Frontier"**
Salem	**Evergreen State**	**Forget-Me-Not**		**Western Meadowlark**

Bingo in the Midwest Region

Teacher Directions:

1. For each player, copy the boxes below on colorful paper. To create each game board, cut apart the boxes, reassemble them into five by five grids in random order, and glue them to card stock. Laminate the game boards for durability.

2. Let each player use a write-on/wipe-away marker to mark her answers as the clues are called. Let the bingo caller use a write-on/wipe-away marker to mark all clues as they are called.

3. Have the caller give oral clues (for example, "the capital of Michigan," or "the state flower of Illinois") for the answers written on the cards.

4. The winner is the first player to correctly cover five boxes in any direction.

☆ Springfield	Buckeye State	Apple Blossom		Tulip Poplar
Robin		Madison	White Pine	Crossroads of America
Scarlet Carnation	Sugar Maple	Wolverine State	Land of Lincoln	☆ Indianapolis
	Native Violet		☆ Columbus	Hoosier State
☆ Lansing	"Forward"	Peony		Cardinal

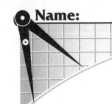

A Puzzled State

Make a crossword puzzle to show information about one of the 50 states.

Materials:
2 Grid patterns (page 67)
Pencil or pen
Marker
2 pieces of notebook paper

Directions:
1. List 10-15 facts about a state. Then, write 10-15 questions using the facts.

2. Create the crossword puzzle answer key by writing the answers to the questions across and down in a typical crossword format on one grid pattern. Outline the used boxes with a marker. Number the answers starting in the upper left part of the grid.

3. On a piece of notebook paper, write the facts in the order they were used in the answer key, separating them into Across and Down categories.

4. On the second grid pattern, outline the boxes that will contain the answers. Number the boxes and color all unused boxes. Use the answer key as a guide.

5. Exchange the puzzle with a classmate to solve.

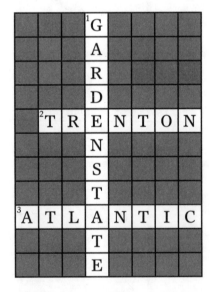

SAMPLE
Across
    2. New Jersey's capital
    3. City with a six-mile boardwalk
Down
    1. Nickname of New Jersey

Activity Extension: To create a state word search puzzle, using the grid pattern (page 67) as a guide, write words associated with a state horizontally, vertically, and diagonally. Have an adult make a copy of this page for the answer key. Then, fill the remaining boxes with random letters. Copy the words from the answer key into a list. Exchange the list and puzzle with a classmate.

Grid Pattern

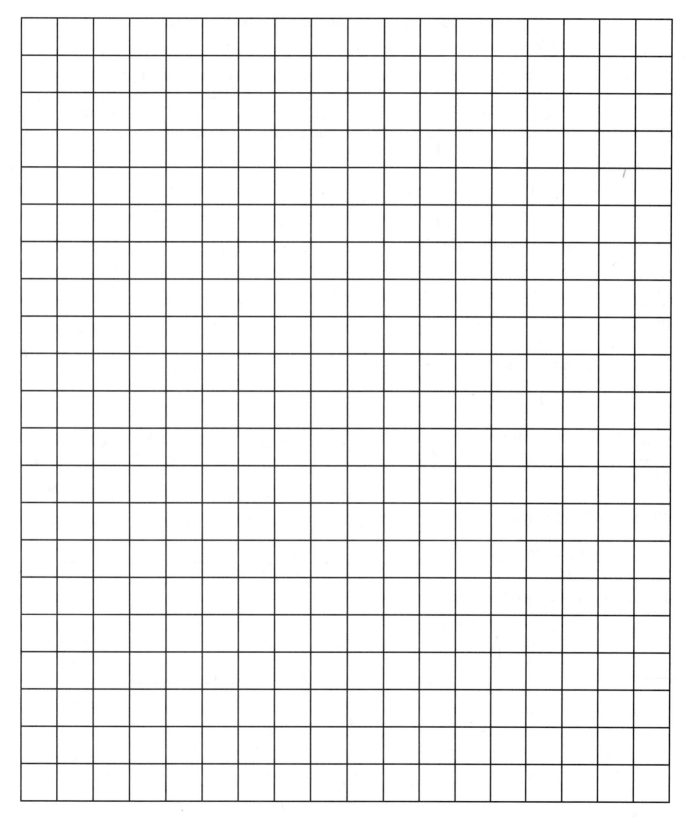

Five Themes Plate

In this activity, a paper plate will serve as the form for a five themes of geography display.

Directions: Research a state. Locate and complete the information on pages 68-69. Then, write the facts from page 68 in the sections on the Circle pattern 2 (page 70). Cut out both Circle patterns and glue them to the front and back of a paper plate. Decorate the outside edge of the plate using the colors in the state's flag.

Location:

Latitude _____   Longitude _____

Bordering states or bodies of water _____

_____

Place:

Landmarks and physical features _____

_____

Capital and major cities _____

Movement:

Number of highways _____

Number of local TV stations _____

Human/Environment Interaction:

Chief crops _____

Minerals _____

Industries _____

Regions:

U.S. Region _____

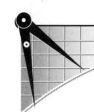

Circle Pattern 1

Draw the state flag.

Tell the meanings of the flag's parts and colors. _____

_____

Draw the shape of the state.

Circle Pattern 2

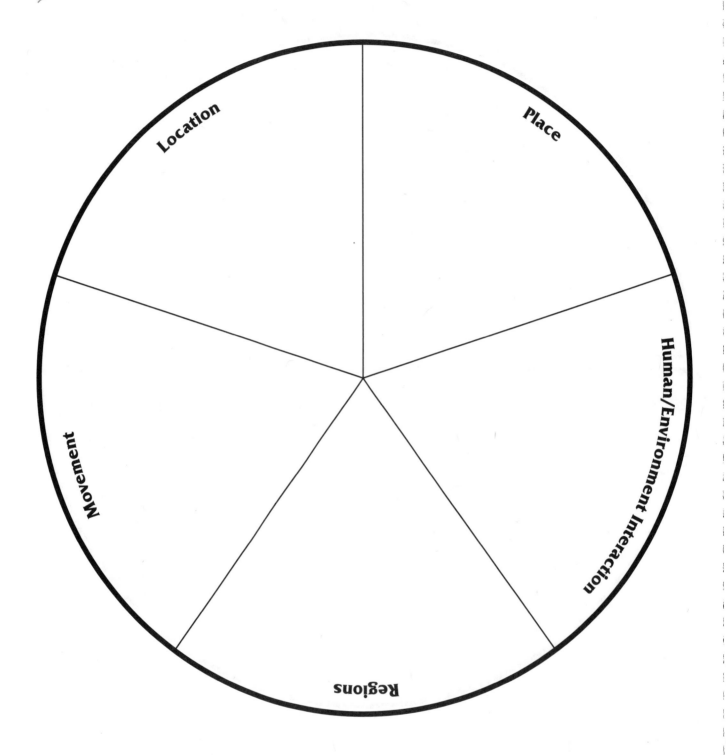

Paper Plate Fact Quiz

Make a paper plate fact quiz to review or test state knowledge.

Materials:
Paper plate
Enlarged copy of question wheel (page 72)
Enlarged copy of circular cover (page 73)
Glue
Markers or colorful pencils
Brass fastener
Scissors

Directions:
1. Research a state. Write 10 short questions and answers from the research.

2. Write one question beside each number on the outer ring of the question wheel. Write the answer to the right of the question on the lines below the next number.

3. Print the name of the state on the circular cover. Then, draw one of the state's symbols, such as the flag, seal, bird, tree, or flower, on the circular cover.

4. Cut out the question wheel and the circular cover.

5. Glue the question wheel to the center of a paper plate.

6. Place the circular cover on the question wheel. Then, insert a brass fastener through the center.

7. Decorate the outside edge of the paper plate with a design suitable for the state.

Question Wheel

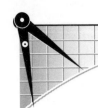

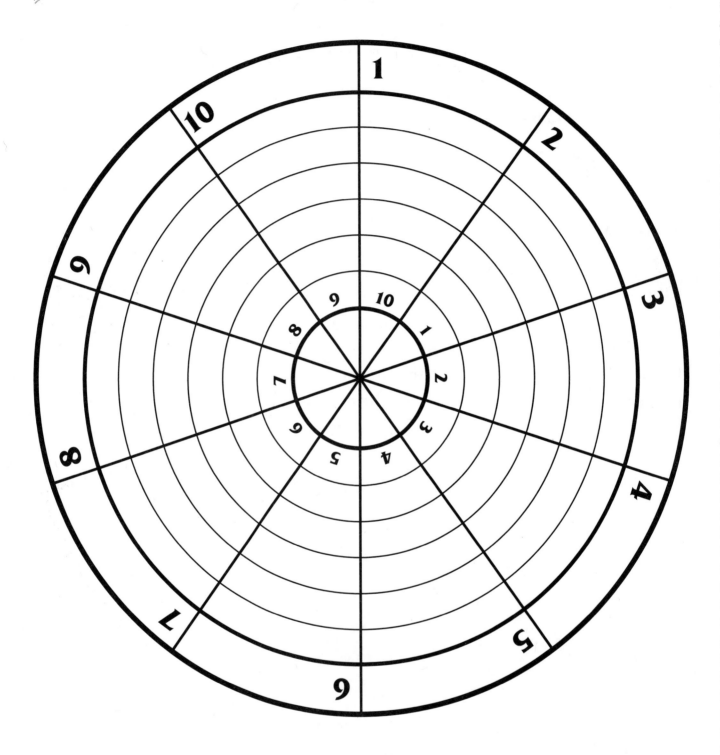

Circular Cover

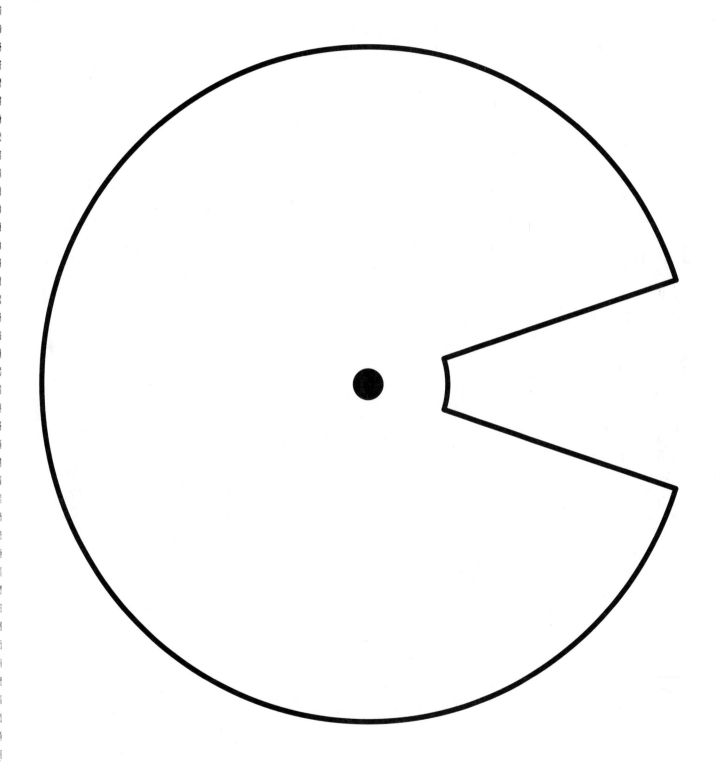

Hitch Your Wagon Book Report

Use the covered wagon pattern to write a book report about an American pioneer.

Directions:

1. Read a book about an American pioneer.

2. On the cover of the wagon (below), describe the places the pioneer traveled, tell about the way(s) the pioneer used the land, and describe the kinds of transportation the pioneer used.

Book's Title: _____   Author: _____

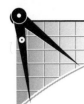

"Geopardy" Game

To the Teacher: This game is a perfect way to review geographical information. It requires some teacher setup, but after the game board has been made, it may be used repeatedly—just add new question cards.

Materials:
Piece of foam board
Markers
30 library pockets
6 clear plastic sleeves
3" x 5" index cards
Glue
Small white boards or chalkboards with erasers
Write-on/wipe-away markers or chalk

Teacher Directions to Make Game Board:
1. Label the top of the foam board with the name *Geopardy*.

2. Attach the library pockets to the foam board in six columns with five library pockets in each column.

3. At the top of each column, glue a clear plastic sleeve.

4. Write the point values on the pockets in each column as follows: 10, 20, 30, 40, and 50, starting at the top and going down. (See the sample game board on page 76.)

5. Choose six geography categories. On six index cards, write the names of the categories. Place these in the clear plastic sleeves.

6. For each category, write five review questions on index cards.

7. On the back of each card, write the category of the question and assign it a point value from 10 to 50 points. (Easier questions should be worth fewer points.)

8. Place the cards in the library pockets according to category and point value, with the review question facing in. Each column should represent one category.

Teacher Directions to Play:
1. Divide the class into small groups.

2. Give each group a small white board, a clean rag, and a write-on/wipe-away marker (or a chalkboard, eraser, and chalk).

3. Have one group choose a category and point value. Read the question and have all of the groups write the answers on their boards. When time is called, have them hold up their answers.

4. Award points to all groups that answered the question correctly.

Sample Game Board

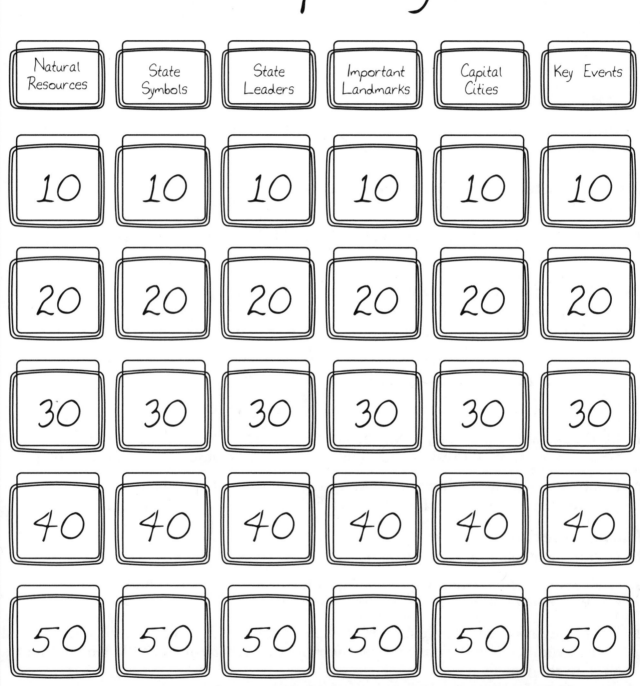

Geopardy

Natural Resources	State Symbols	State Leaders	Important Landmarks	Capital Cities	Key Events
10	10	10	10	10	10
20	20	20	20	20	20
30	30	30	30	30	30
40	40	40	40	40	40
50	50	50	50	50	50

Native American Map

Learn about the Native American cultural groups and the tribes within them.

Materials: 3" x 5" index cards, markers, yarn, pushpins

Directions:

1. The class will be divided into eight groups, each representing one of the Native American cultural groups: Southwest, Southeast, California, Great Basin, Northwest Coast, Eastern Woodlands, Plains, and Plateau. As a group, choose one or more tribes within the cultural group to research.

2. Write five important facts about the tribes on index cards.

3. Place the index cards around a posted enlarged copy of the map below.

4. Using a length of yarn and pushpins, connect each card to the location of the corresponding tribe.

Activity Extension: On a separate sheet of paper, make a chart listing the eight Native American cultural groups. Under each group's name, list the tribes in that group.

A Daring Diorama

Here is a hands-on activity to make a model of a Native American village.

Materials:

Shoe box   Assorted colors of construction paper
Modeling clay   Wooden dowels or craft sticks
Scissors   Variety of beads and feathers
Glue   Markers
Fabric scraps

Directions:

1. Choose a Native American tribe to research. Find out about the housing, climate, landforms, and village life of the tribe.

2. Cover the outside of the shoe box with tan construction paper.

3. Create a background scene inside of the box that represents the area where the tribe lived. Cut out shapes from different colors of construction paper, use markers to draw pictures, and/or form structures from modeling clay.

4. Make a model of the type of shelter used by the tribe. Use clay for pueblos, brown construction paper and wooden dowels for tepees, or craft sticks for lodges.

5. Using clay, make a model of a Native American Indian who represents the tribe. Make clothing from fabric scraps and beads and feathers, as appropriate.

6. Assemble the parts of the diorama into a village scene.

Creating a Mask

The Iroquois from the eastern Great Lakes made a variety of masks. A famous type was the wooden masks of the False Face Society. The False Face masks were used during healing ceremonies to drive away illnesses. The masks were carved from living trees. When a mask was almost finished, it was cut away from the tree. If a mask was started in the morning, it was painted red. If it was started in the afternoon, it was painted black. Some masks were painted half red and half black.

Materials:
9" x 12" poster board
Large, heavy-duty paper plate
Masking tape
Pencil
Scissors
Papier-mâché paste
2" x 8" newspaper strips
Craft paint (red or black)
Craft paintbrushes
Other craft materials (optional)

Directions:
1. Fold the poster board in half. To make a nose, draw a 3" line from the top of the fold downward at an angle. From that point, draw a straight line to the center fold.

2. On the edge opposite of the fold, draw an ear shape.

3. Leaving the poster board folded, cut on the lines to make two ears and one nose.

4. Using masking tape, attach the ears to the edge of a paper plate. (Note: the back of the paper plate will be the face of the mask.) Place a piece of tape on each side of the nose and attach it to the center of the plate.

5. Dip newspaper strips into papier-mâché paste and lay the strips across the nose. Make sure there are no air bubbles under the strips.

6. Continue laying the strips to cover the nose and then the ears. With the remaining strips, cover the rest of the plate. Allow the strips to dry.

7. Research additional information about False Face masks. Use craft paint and other craft materials to create additional facial features or designs.

"Canoe" Tell the Facts?

Many Native Americans relied on transportation by water. Canoes were often made of bark, which made them lightweight and easy to carry. These canoes were made by fastening bark to a wooden frame. Dugout canoes were made from hollowed out tree trunks. Some of the larger dugout canoes could carry as many as 60 people.

Materials:

Scissors   Markers or colorful pencils
Hole punch   Brown yarn

Directions:

1. Research to find a Native American tribe that used canoes. Find out the ways that the canoes were built and how they were used.

2. Cut out the canoe pattern below.

3. List several canoe facts on the canoe's sides. Then, color and decorate the canoe.

4. Fold the canoe along the dashed line. Punch out the holes along the border. Then, lace the sides together with brown yarn.

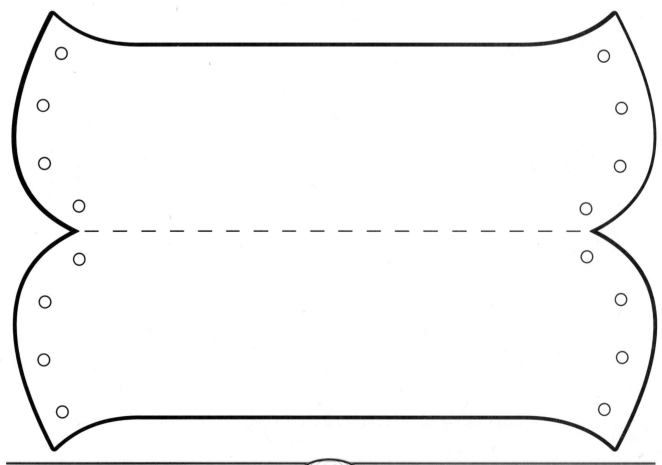

Great Explorers Playlist

Design a CD playlist that includes interesting facts about an explorer.

Directions: Choose an explorer from the list below. In the center of the CD, write the name of the explorer and your name. Research to find information in the categories listed on the CD. Then, fill in the sections of the CD with the facts.

Explorers:

Vasco Núñez de Balboa
Sir Francis Drake
John Cabot
Leif Eriksson
Samuel de Champlain

Henry Hudson
William Clark
Robert Cavelier sieur
  de La Salle
Christopher Columbus

Meriwether Lewis
Hernán Cortés
Ferdinand Magellan
Hernando de Soto
Juan Ponce de León

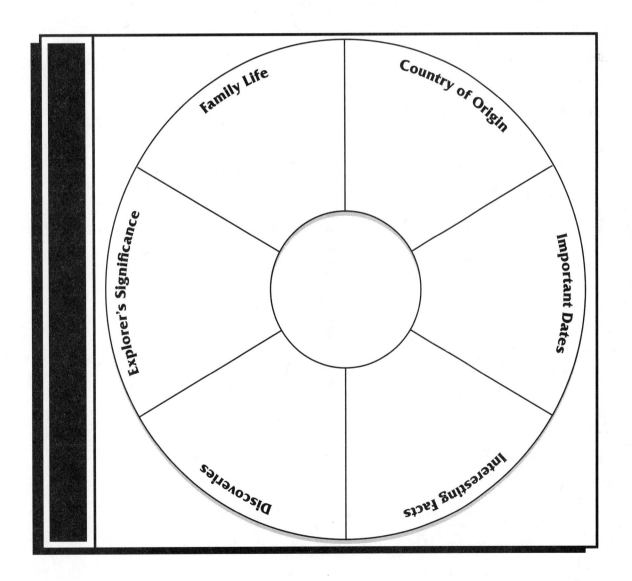

A "Timely" Activity

Here is a way to conveniently summarize and display facts about an explorer's life and adventures.

Materials:

4" x 6" index cards	Markers
Poster board	Construction paper
Scissors	Glue

Directions:

1. Research an explorer. Take notes about important dates and events that occurred during the explorer's lifetime.

2. On each index card, record one date and the corresponding event.

3. Arrange the cards in chronological order.

4. Decide on a picture that best represents the explorer's life. Draw a large outline of the picture on a piece of poster board, then cut it out.

5. Attach the index cards in the correct order to make a time line around the picture outline.

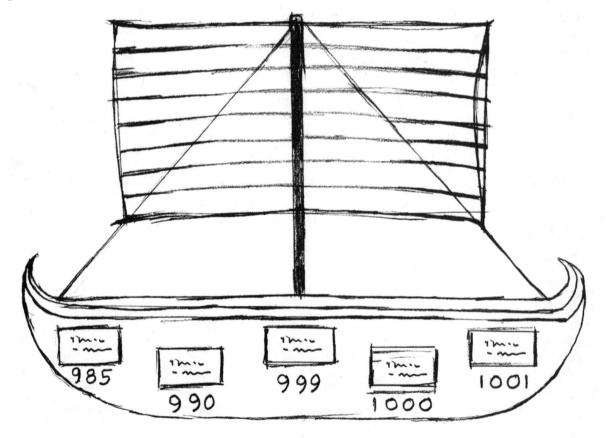

Can-It Colonies

To the Teacher: When learning about the 13 original colonies, here is a fun way to store facts about each of them. If possible, divide the class into 13 groups to represent the colonies.

Materials:
Can with plastic lid (such as a cleaned coffee, potato chip, or peanut can)
Construction paper
Markers
Tape
3" x 8" paper strips
Scissors

Directions:

1. Research a colony.

2. Record important facts about the colony (the date it was founded, its leaders, important historical events, the area's natural resources, etc.) on paper strips.

3. Wrap the can with construction paper and trim to fit. Then, lay the paper flat and use markers to decorate it with the colony's flag, motto, or other pictures that represent the colony. Finally, attach the paper to the can with tape.

4. Fill the can with the fact strips.

5. Exchange cans with other groups to learn about the other colonies. As a class, make a list of similarities and differences between the 13 original colonies.

An Explorer's Notebook

As a class, create a library of notebooks about famous explorers.

Materials:
Notebook paper
6 sheets of white paper
Pencil or pen
Glass of tea
String or yarn
Poster board
Yarn
Hole punch

Directions:

1. Research an explorer. Record notes on notebook paper about the explorer's preparations and his travels.

2. After collecting the information, sprinkle each piece of white paper with tea to make it look old. Allow the pages to dry.

3. Use the notes to create the following pages: title page, map(s) of the voyage(s), want ad to recruit the crew, public announcement about the journey, letter to the monarch who is funding the exploration, and list of the voyage's results.

4. After completing the pages, further "age" them by carefully crumpling each sheet of paper, then spreading it out again.

5. Assemble the pages in order according to Step 3.

6. Make a cover from two small pieces of poster board. Repeat the aging process in Steps 2 and 4. Then, punch holes in the covers and pages. Bind the book together with a piece of yarn.

Explorers' Journal

Meriwether Lewis and William Clark made many discoveries. Known as Lewis and Clark, these two men are often considered the greatest explorers of America. President Thomas Jefferson asked Lewis and Clark to complete five main tasks on their expedition: to follow the largest river west to the Pacific Ocean, to cross the Rocky Mountains, to find the source of the Missouri River, to begin trade with the native people, and to let the Native Americans know about the peaceful intentions of the United States. Their difficult expedition began on May 14, 1804, and lasted 28 months, covering more than 8,000 miles. Meriwether Lewis had five years of schooling while William Clark only received some tutoring from his older brothers. In their journal entries, the many spelling mistakes and errors in grammar show their lack of formal education.

Materials:
Journal entries (pages 86-87)
2 sheets of white paper
1 sheet of construction paper
Markers or colorful pencils
Scissors
Glue
Yarn or string
Hole punch

Directions:

1. Cut apart the eight journal entries. Place them in chronological order.

2. Fold two pieces of white paper in half lengthwise to create eight journal pages.

3. Glue one journal entry to each journal page in the correct order.

4. Read each of the journal entries and think about the discoveries Lewis and Clark made and the adventures they had.

5. Draw a picture to go with each journal entry.

6. Fold the construction paper lengthwise to make a cover for the journal.

7. Punch holes in the left side of the cover and journal pages. Bind the journal together with a piece of string or yarn.

8. Label the cover "Lewis and Clark's Journal."

Journal Entries

January 4, 1806

These people have been very friendly to us; they appear to be a mild, inoffensive people, but will pilfer if they have an opportunity . . . they are great higlers in trade.

– Meriwether Lewis

November 11, 1804

Continued work at the fort. Two men cut themselves with an ax. The large ducks pass to the South. An Indian gave me several rolls of parched meat.

– William Clark

June 14, 1805

. . . and having entirely forgotten to reload my rifle, a large white, or reather brown bear, had perceived and crept on me within 20 steps before I discovered him;
. . . I drew up my gun to shoot but in the same instant I recolected that she was not loaded . . . I had no sooner terned myself about but he pitched at me. I ran about 80 yards and found he gained on me fast. I then run into the water.

– Meriwether Lewis

May 14, 1805
The whol face of the country was covered with herds of Buffaloe, Elk, and Antelopes; deer are also abundant, but keep themselves more concealed in the woodland. The buffaloe Elk and Antelope are so gentle that we pass near them while feeding without apearing to excite any alarm; and when we attract their attention, they frequently approach us to discover what we are.

– Meriwether Lewis

Journal Entries

January 15, 1804

My situation is as comfortable as could be expected in the woods . . . the Missouri which mouths imedeately opposet is the river we intend assending . . .

– William Clark

July 6, 1806

The little animal found in the plains of the Missouri which I have called the barking squirrel weighs from 3 to 3½ pounds. it's colour is an uniform light brick red grey. The legs are short, the head is also bony muscular and stout . . . the upper lip is split or divided to the nose. the ears are short.

– Meriwether Lewis

May 26, 1805

I beheld the Rocky Mountains for the first time. When I reflected on the difficulty which snowey barrier would most probably throw in my way to the Pacific . . . it in some measure counterballanced the joy I had felt in the first few minutes I gazed at them.

– Meriwether Lewis

April 7, 1805

We are now about to penetrate a country at least 2,000 miles in width, on which the foot of civilized man had never trodden . . . Entertaining as I do, the most confident hope of succeading in a voyage which had formed a darling project of mine for the last ten years.

– Meriwether Lewis

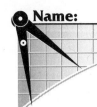

Come to My Colony

In the space below, design a magazine ad to entice Europeans to come to one of the 13 original colonies.

Directions:

Research one of the 13 original colonies. Based on the facts you discover, design a magazine ad encouraging other potential settlers to visit the colony. Include information about its location, natural resources, or interesting features.

Let Freedom Ring Report

There are many people who worked hard to create the United States and provide the freedoms available today. Some of these patriots gave their lives for these freedoms. One recognizable symbol of these freedoms is the Liberty Bell.

Materials:

Glitter glue   Bell pattern (page 90)
Red, white, or blue ribbon   Pen or pencil
Scissors   Hole punch

Directions:

1. Research an American patriot listed below. Find a quotation by or about that person.

2. Write a one-paragraph report about the famous patriot on the bell pattern. Include the quotation in the report, giving the details of when, where, and why it was said.

3. Cut out the bell and decorate the back with glitter glue.

4. Punch a hole in the top. Then, string a piece of red, white, or blue ribbon through the hole to display the finished report.

Famous American Patriots

Abigail Adams   Thomas Jefferson
John Adams   John Paul Jones
Samuel Adams   Sybil Ludington
Ethan Allen   Dolley Madison
Crispus Attucks   James Madison
George Rogers Clark   James Monroe
Benjamin Franklin   Thomas Paine
Nathanael Greene   Paul Revere
Nathan Hale   Betsy Ross
Patrick Henry   Deborah Sampson
John Jay   George Washington

Bell Pattern

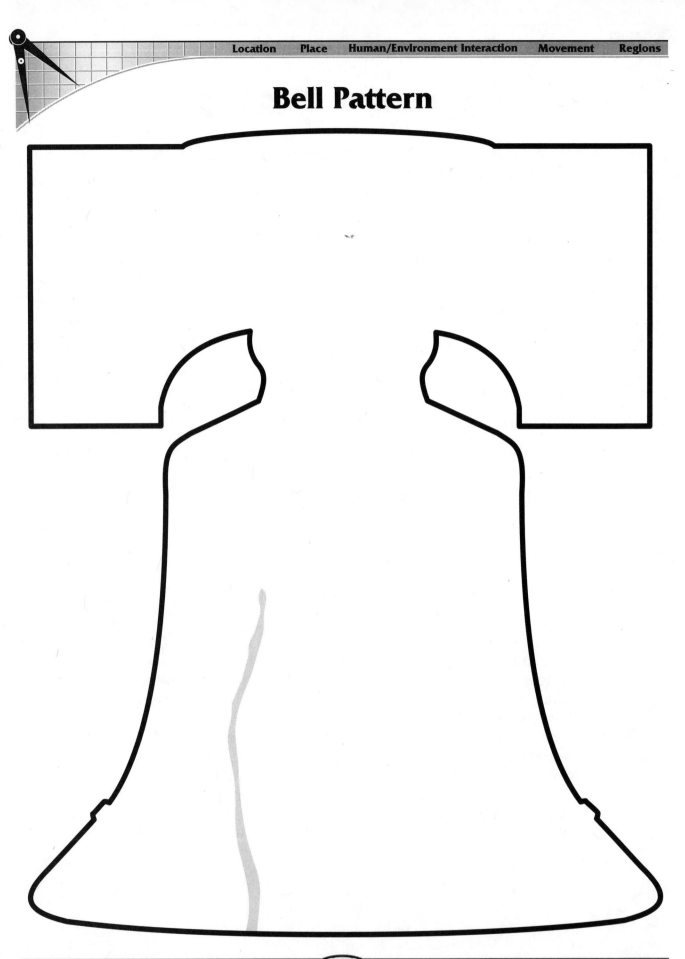

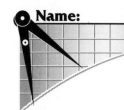

Colonial Clothing

In this activity, discover the fashions of the colonial period.

Materials:

Glue   People outlines (below)

Scissors   Colorful paper or fabric scraps

Markers or colorful pencils

Directions: Research the type of clothing worn during the colonial period, including the colors and types of fabric. Draw the clothing on the outlines or cut clothing from colorful paper or fabric scraps and glue it to the outlines.

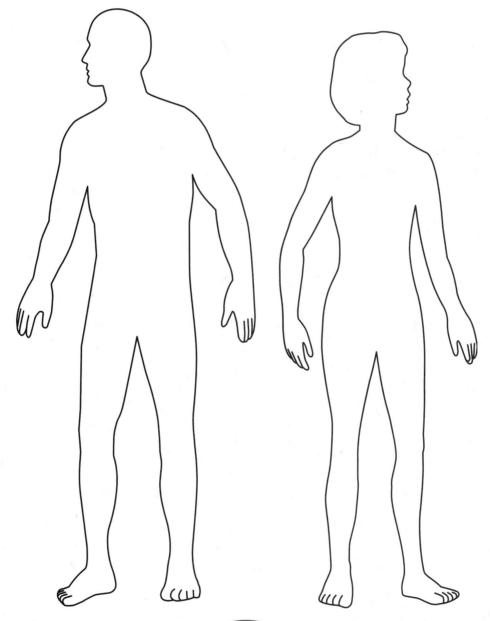

Secret Messages

During times of war, people on both sides want to keep information secret from each other. This was true during the Revolutionary War. Many times, mail was intercepted by either the British or the American Patriots. In order to keep messages secret, different ways were devised to hide them. One strategy was writing with invisible ink.

Materials:

Lemon juice   Small bowl

Cotton swab   Notebook paper

Lamp

Directions:

1. Pour a few teaspoons of lemon juice into a bowl.

2. Dip a cotton swab into the lemon juice.

3. With the dipped end of the cotton swab, write a secret message on a piece of notebook paper.

4. When the writing has dried, have an adult help hold the back of the paper close to a hot lightbulb. The message will become visible as the paper heats.

Patriotic Pyramid

Create a patriotic pyramid to wrap up the study of the American Revolution.

Materials:

Pyramid pattern (page 94)   Glue
White poster board   3 sheets of construction paper in assorted colors
Scissors   Markers or colorful pencils

Directions:

1. Research a patriot to find information about her life, a quotation, a time line, and a picture.

2. Glue the pyramid pattern to a piece of white poster board. Then, cut out the pyramid.

3. Trace one side of the pyramid onto three pieces of construction paper and cut out.

4. Glue the construction paper triangles to the sides of the pyramid.

5. Write information about the patriot's life on Side 1.

6. On Side 2, write a quotation by or about the patriot.

7. On Side 3, draw a picture of the patriot. If a picture cannot be found or drawn, write a time line of the patriot's life.

8. To assemble the pyramid, fold on the dashed lines and glue the tabs to the sides of the pyramid.

Pyramid Pattern

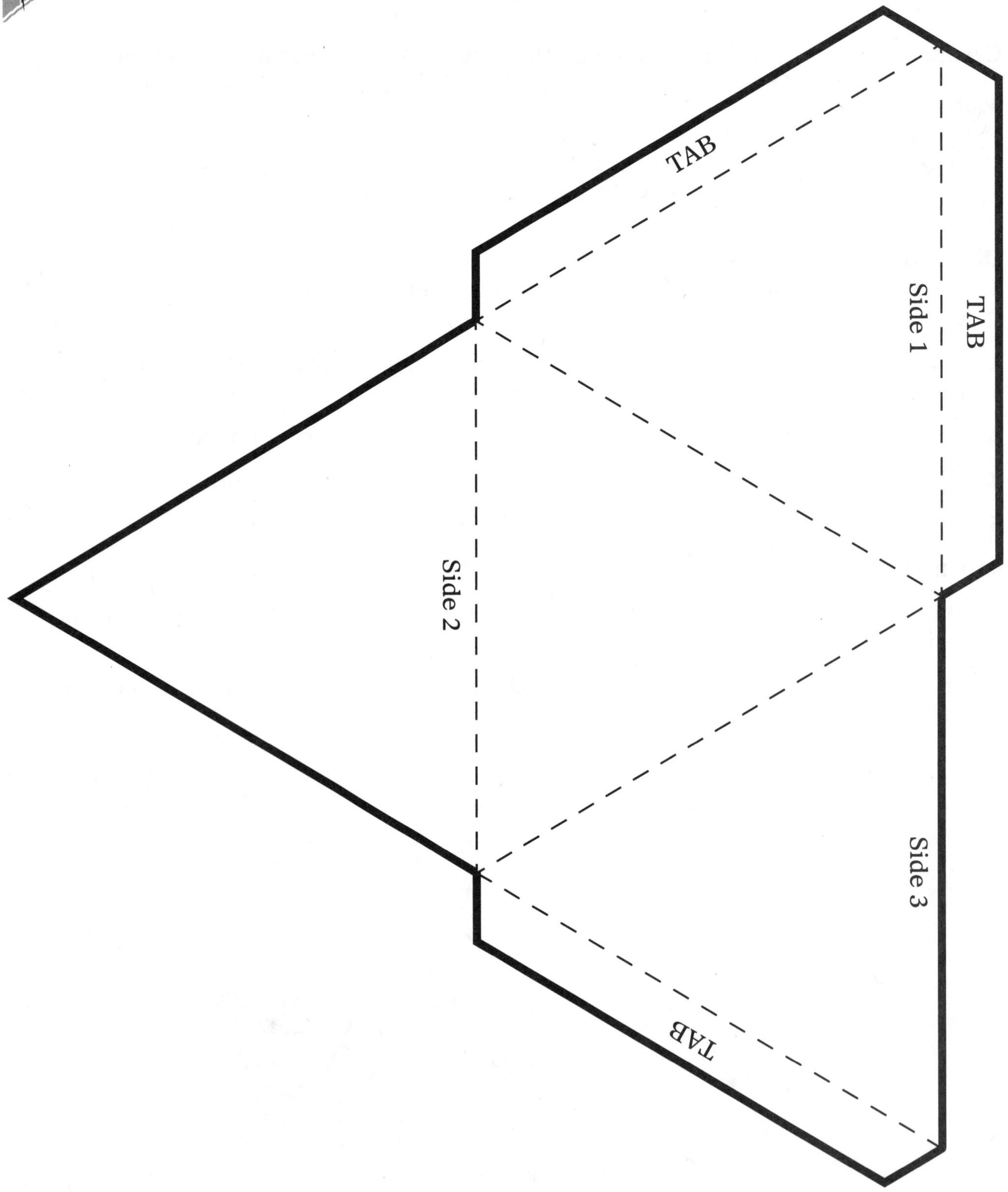

TAB

Side 1

TAB

Side 2

Side 3

TAB

Whodunit?

Who invented the lightbulb? Where did peanut butter come from? Who invented the elevator? Inventors are responsible for the many amazing ideas and inventions used today.

Directions: Review the list below and choose one of the inventors to research. Use the Whodunit? worksheet on page 96 to complete a report.

Inventors

Benjamin Banneker
Alexander Graham Bell
Rachel Carson
George Washington Carver
Luther Crowell
Thomas Edison
Henry Ford
Robert Fulton
King Gillette
Walter Hunt
Whitcomb Judson
John Loud
Garrett Morgan
Samuel F. B. Morse
Dr. James Naismith
Alfred Nobel
Elisha Otis
John Stith Pemberton
Jacob Schick
Ruth Wakefield
Madam C. J. Walker
Eli Whitney
Wilbur and Orville Wright

Whodunit?

Inventor's Name: _____

Invention/Idea: _____

Invention's/Idea's Function: _____

_____

How did this invention/idea help improve people's lives? _____

_____

_____

_____

What process did the inventor use to develop the invention/idea? _____

_____

_____

_____

Draw a picture of the invention/idea in action.

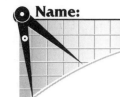
Inventive Characters

Using the light bulb pattern below, work as a class to create a bulletin board display featuring various American inventors.

Materials: scissors, markers or colorful pencils, yarn, pushpins

Directions:

1. On the pattern below, write an American inventor's name and the invention for which he is most famous. Cut out the lightbulb.

2. Display the lightbulb beside a posted U.S. map.

3. Connect the lightbulb to the location in the United States where the inventor lived using a piece of yarn and pushpins.

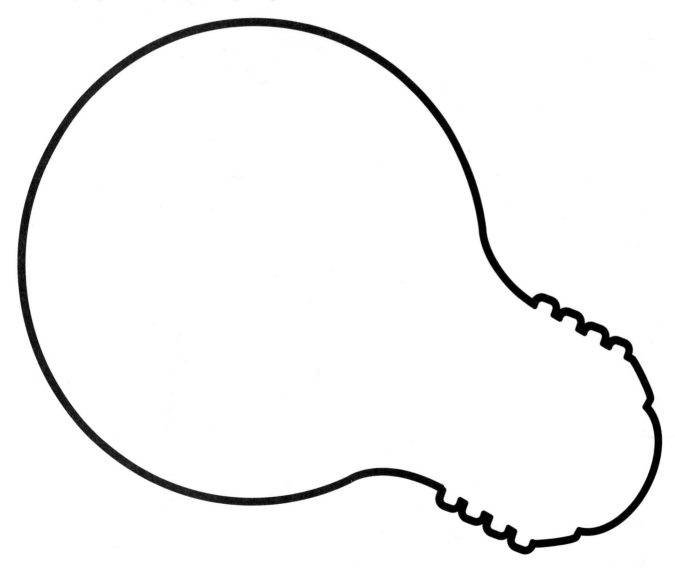

Letter from My New Home

This activity combines American History knowledge with persuasion skills.

Directions: Pretend it is 1776. In the space below, write a convincing letter to your parents in England about why they should let you stay and work in America.

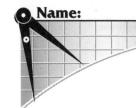

Reports in "Ship-Shape"

After completing this activity, post your report with your classmates' to make a bulletin board display titled "Set Sail with American History!"

Materials: scissors, glue, markers or colorful pencils, colorful construction paper

Directions:

1. Select a book on one of the following American history topics: explorers, colonies, patriots, Native Americans, or inventors.

2. After reading the book, write a report on the ship pattern below.

3. Color and cut out the ship. Then, glue it to a sheet of colorful construction paper to form a frame.

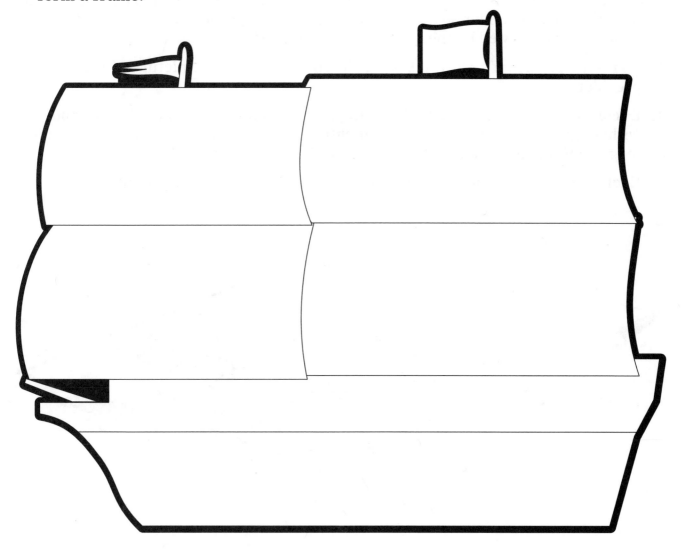

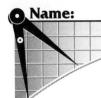
Name That President

Here's an idea to build intrigue and interest while learning about U.S. presidents.

Materials:
Colorful file folders
Markers or colorful pencils
Pens
Glue
Scissors

Directions:
1. Research a U.S. president. Find six important facts.

2. Write clues about the facts on the outside of a colorful file folder. The clues should be written on the folder so that the folder opens at the bottom. Write the clues in first person, followed by the question, "Who Am I?"

3. Write the president's name inside of the folder and draw a picture of the president.

4. Decorate the outside of the folder with pictures that pertain to the U.S. president without giving away the president's identity. Draw the pictures or cut them from magazines and glue them to the outside of the file folder.

5. Exchange folders with classmates to learn about other U.S. presidents.

Presidents Making a Mark

Create a bookmark containing key presidential facts to serve as a reminder of important information.

Materials:

Pens   Hole punch
Scissors   Red, white, and blue ribbons
Glue   Markers or colorful pencils
Contact paper

Directions:

1. Research a U.S. president and fill in the information on the bookmark patterns below. Then, decorate the edges of the bookmarks.

2. Cut out the bookmark patterns and glue them back-to-back.

3. Cover the bookmark with clear contact paper. Punch a hole where indicated.

4. String thin red, white, and blue ribbons through the hole and tie to form a tassel.

Previous Position

Accomplishments

Term(s) in Office

Other Notable Fact

Name

Place of Birth

Date of Birth

Family Background

Education

Reading, Interpreting, and Creating Charts

A **chart** is a visual tool that provides a simple way to see information. Reading and interpreting the data found in charts is an essential skill for students to learn. The next few pages contain activities to help students practice this skill.

The following chart activity was developed from information about the 13 original colonies. Copy the Thirteen Colonies chart (page 103) and Thirteen Colonies questions (page 104) for each student. Have students work in pairs or small groups to answer the questions. Then, have students use the Create a Chart (page 105) to create their own charts with information about different states.

When using the sample chart on page 103, point out the following details about the chart to students.

- **Date Started:** On the chart, notice that Connecticut's and North Carolina's dates are written as c. 1635 and c. 1653. The "c" stands for the word *circa*, which means approximately or about. All other founding dates are exact.

- **Founded By:** Notice that some colonies were founded by individuals; other colonies were founded by groups or companies.

- **Became a Royal Colony:** Some, but not all, of the colonies became royal colonies.

- **Population in 1740:** Population is an estimation based on the statistics taken from population censuses, vital statistics registration, or from sample surveys.

Thirteen Colonies Chart

Directions: Use this chart to answer the questions on page 104.

Name	Date Started	Founded By	Became a Royal Colony	Population in 1740
Connecticut	c. 1635	Thomas Hooker		90,000
Delaware	1638	Peter Minuit and New Sweden Company		20,000
Georgia	1732	James Edward Oglethorpe	1752	2,000
Maryland	1634	Lord Baltimore		116,000
Massachusetts	1620	Puritans	1691	152,000
New Hampshire	1623	John Wheelwright	1679	23,000
New Jersey	1660	Lord Berkeley and Sir George Carteret	1702	51,000
New York	1626	Duke of York	1685	64,000
North Carolina	c. 1653	Virginians	1729	52,000
Pennsylvania	1682	William Penn		86,000
Rhode Island	1636	Roger Williams		25,000
South Carolina	1670	Eight nobles with a royal charter from Charles II	1729	45,000
Virginia	1607	London Company	1624	180,000

Thirteen Colonies Chart

Directions: Answer the following questions using the chart on page 103.

1. Which colonies had the largest populations in 1740?

   _____   _____

   _____   _____

   _____

2. List the colonies that had the smallest populations in 1740.

   _____   _____

   _____   _____

3. Which colonies were founded by companies?

   _____   _____

4. Which colonies were started by 1638?

   _____   _____

   _____   _____

   _____   _____

   _____

5. Which colonies did not become royal colonies?

   _____   _____

   _____   _____

   _____

6. Which colonies were founded by one or two individuals?

   _____   _____

   _____   _____

   _____   _____

   _____

7. Name the colonies that had more than 100,000 people in 1740.

   _____   _____

   _____

Create a Chart

Directions: Create a chart using current information about 13 different states. After gathering the facts, compare and contrast the findings below.

State	Region	Capital	Population	Area (Sq. Miles)

Findings: _____

_____

_____

_____

_____

Reading, Interpreting, and Creating Graphs

A **graph** can be defined as a visual tool that allows a person to see and use information. The ability to read and interpret graphs is an important skill for students to learn. The following graph activities are designed to improve critical thinking skills, such as summarizing information, drawing conclusions, and interpreting and analyzing data.

There are four main types of graphs: **pictograph**, **circle**, **bar**, and **line**. Sometimes a graph includes a key to identify vital information that is represented by symbols on the graph. Introduce the graphs on pages 106 and 107 that show the populations of four U.S. cities. Point out to students that the same information can be shown in different ways on different graphs.

A **pictograph** uses pictures instead of numbers, bars, or lines. Pictographs are visually pleasing. Much of the numerical information is easily displayed and can be compared at a glance.

Populations of Four U.S. Cities

City	Population
New York	● ● ● ● ● ● ● ●
Los Angeles	● ● ● ●
Chicago	● ● ●
Dallas	●

Reading, Interpreting, and Creating Graphs

Another type of informational graph is a **circle graph** or a **pie graph**. In this type of graph, things can be divided into the parts or percentages of a whole. All parts must add up to be a whole, or 100%. Think of the pieces of an entire pie. Together, the pieces must add up to a whole pie.

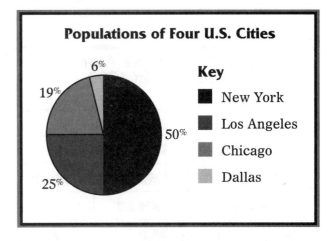

Bar graphs display numerical information by the height or length of parallel bars. The bars may be drawn either vertically or horizontally—the way the bars are drawn depends on what is being shown. One type of bar graph uses single bars. Another type of bar graph uses more than one bar to show comparisons of two or more things.

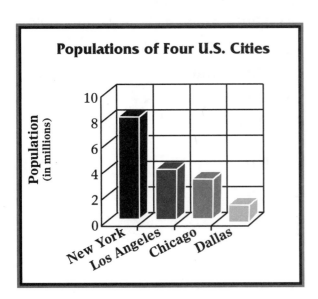

A **line graph** uses dots that are connected by lines to show changes and to compare information over time. When comparing two or more different things on a line graph, use a different color or type of line for each thing.

American Colonies Graph

Directions: After studying the graph below, answer the questions.

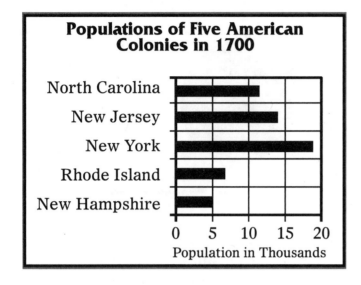

Populations of Five American Colonies in 1700

North Carolina
New Jersey
New York
Rhode Island
New Hampshire

0   5   10   15   20
Population in Thousands

1. Which of these colonies had the smallest population in 1700?

    A. North Carolina
    B. New York
    C. Rhode Island
    D. New Hampshire

2. North Carolina had about _____ as many people as New Hampshire.

    A. twice
    B. three times
    C. four times
    D. half

3. Which of these colonies had the most people in 1700?

    A. New Jersey
    B. Rhode Island
    C. New York
    D. North Carolina

4. New Hampshire had about _____ people in 1700.

    A. 5,000
    B. 5,000,000
    C. 50,000
    D. 500,000

5. The population of these two colonies together is about the same as that of the colony of North Carolina.

    A. Rhode Island and New York
    B. New Hampshire and North Carolina
    C. New York and New Hampshire
    D. Rhode Island and New Hampshire

Create a Bar Graph

Directions: Conduct a poll. Ask each person to choose which of the following vacation destinations she would rather visit during the summer: **amusement park, camp, beach, mountains,** or **national park**. Graph your results on the blank bar graph below.

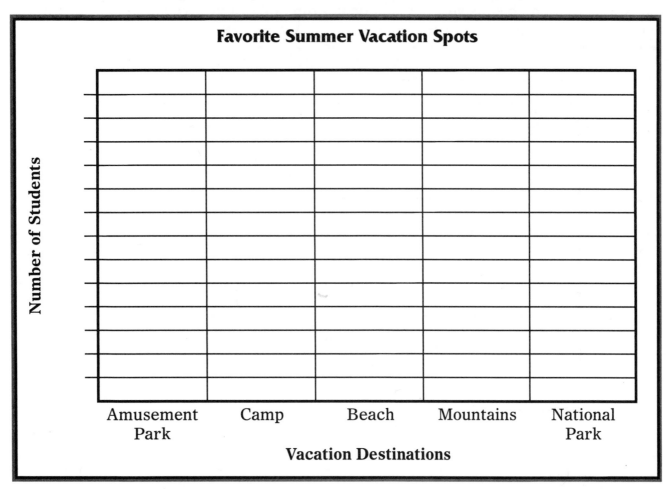

Favorite Summer Vacation Spots

Number of Students

Amusement Park   Camp   Beach   Mountains   National Park

Vacation Destinations

Create a Line Graph

Directions: Interview students in your grade level to find out their bedtimes over the course of five years. Record students' responses. Create a line graph to show the results on the blank graph below. After completing the line graph, write three questions that can be answered by analyzing the line graph. Exchange your graph with a classmate and answer the questions.

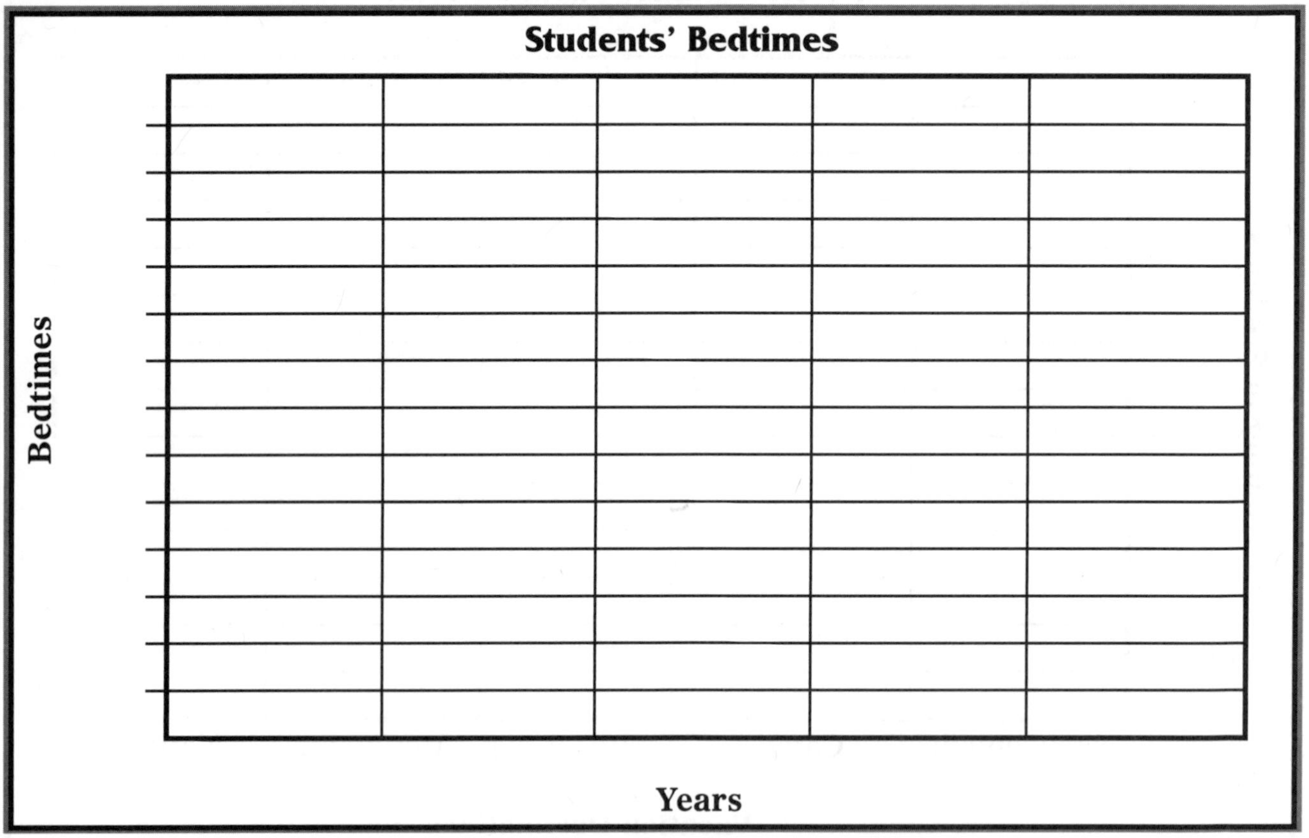

Students' Bedtimes

Bedtimes

Years

Key

1. _____

_____

2. _____

_____

3. _____

_____

Create a Circle Graph

Directions: Conduct two surveys—one of students and one of adults. Ask each person to name his favorite ice cream flavor. Record the results of the survey, then create two circle graphs, one showing student preferences and the other showing adult preferences. Include a key for each graph.

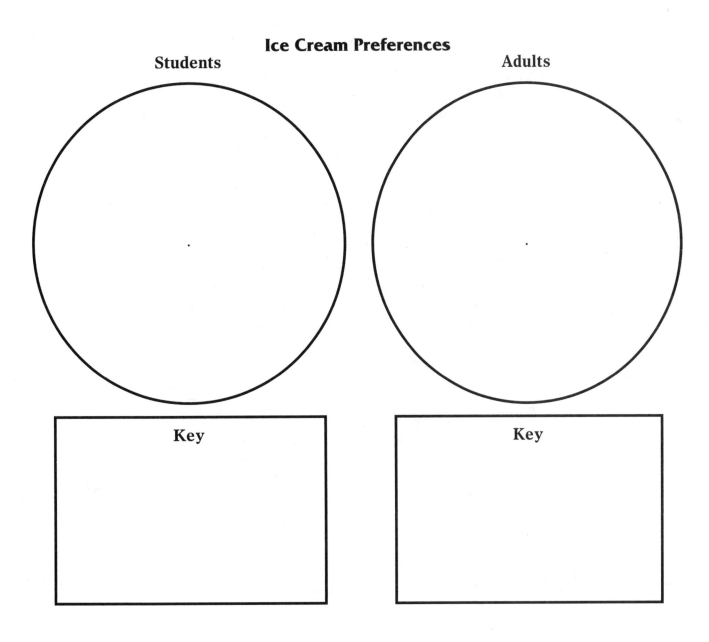

Ice Cream Preferences

Students   Adults

Key   Key

Reading, Interpreting, and Creating Diagrams

Diagrams are clearly drawn pictures with labels. The labels enable someone reading the diagram to easily identify the parts of what is pictured. A diagram can also show information about how something is put together. Diagrams help explain where things are, how things are made, what things do, or even how things grow. Some examples of different kinds of diagrams are flowcharts, Venn diagrams, organizational charts, family trees, and picture diagrams.

Diagrams are helpful in teaching students how to process, organize, and prioritize new information. They also help students clarify their thinking. Diagrams reveal patterns and step-by-step processes. Diagrams can also stimulate creative thinking.

Diagrams can be very useful because they do the following:

- give the reader important information quickly

- help the reader understand what a writer is explaining

- expand on written information with visuals

Use the example below to demonstrate for students how to read and interpret diagrams.

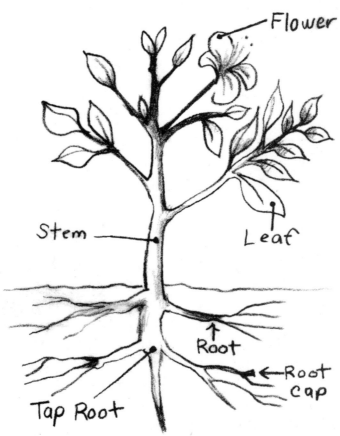

Diagram: Conestoga Wagon

Directions: Look at the diagrams of the Conestoga wagon, also known as the prairie schooner. Study the diagrams and read the information below. Then, answer the questions on page 114.

The three main parts of a prairie schooner were the **cover**, the **wagon bed**, and the **undercarriage**.

The cover usually was made of cotton or canvas. A frame of hickory bows held up the cover and was tied to each side of the wagon bed. The cover extended beyond the bows and could be closed with drawstrings.

The wagon bed was usually about 4 feet wide and 10-12 feet long. It was shaped like a rectangular wooden box. At the front end, there was a compartment called a jockey box that held tools.

The undercarriage included the wheels, which were covered with iron, an axle assembly that connected each pair of wheels, and the reach that connected the two axle assemblies. Fastened to the rear axle and the reach were the hounds, which also connected to the wagon tongue and the front axle. A grease bucket hung from the rear axle and contained a mixture of tar and tallow used to lubricate the wheels.

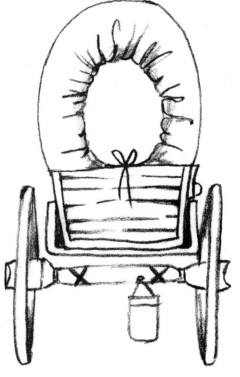

Diagram: Conestoga Wagon

Directions: Use the information and diagrams on page 113 to answer the questions.

1. About how long was the wagon bed? _____

2. What connected each pair of wheels? _____

3. Name two types of fabric that were used to make the cover of the wagon.

    _____

4. What was another name for the Conestoga wagon? _____

5. What held up the cover of the wagon? _____

6. List the three parts of the undercarriage.

    _____

7. What mixture was used to lubricate the wheels? _____

8. Name the part that held the tools. _____

9. How was the cover closed? _____

10. Why do you think the cover might need to be closed?

    _____

11. If you were traveling in a Conestoga wagon, what things might you have tied to
    the side of the wagon? Why?

    _____

    _____

    _____

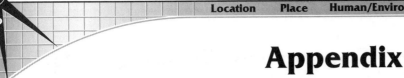
Appendix

Assessment Rubrics:

A **rubric** is a form of assessment that describes the range of a student's performance. A rubric can have several levels of performance or perhaps just two or three. It contains an average level and levels both above and below the average to describe either exemplary or weak performances. Good rubrics are designed carefully to assess the chosen skills. These rubrics match the work that they will measure. Students should be made aware of a rubric's criteria before completing a project that will be graded using the rubric. Pages 116-121 contain sample rubrics.

Tips for Creating a Rubric:

- A rubric should evaluate what was actually taught.

- The rubric should fit a wide range of student abilities.

- Choose which category will be used for ranking student performance.

- Keep in mind the requirements for successful student performance.

- Each level should give a label or numerical score to define a different degree of success or mastery.

Tips for Scoring a Rubric:

- Refer to the rubric frequently when scoring a student's performance or work.

- Focus only on the rubric's criteria to avoid comparing students' papers.

- Decide what points or grades will correspond with the rankings on the rubric.

Graphic Organizers:

A **graphic organizer** is a tool used to illustrate students' knowledge about a topic. Pages 122-125 contain reproducible generic graphic organizers.

National Geography Standards:

The National Geography Standards were written by the National Council for Geographic Education whose goal is to produce a geographically informed person who sees meaning in the arrangement of things in space and applies a spatial perspective to life situations.* Page 126 contains these standards.

*Source: National Council for Geographic Education, http://www.ncge.org (accessed June 2005).

Three-Point Geography Project Rubric

Name: _____   Class: _____

Project Title: _____   Date: _____

Grading Scale: This geography project will receive a score of 3, 2, or 1 to describe the effort, amount of knowledge, and degree of understanding demonstrated in its completion.

❸ This geography project shows a complete understanding of the key concepts. All five themes of geography are presented appropriately. The visual aid is neat, colorful, and attractive. All words are spelled correctly, and communication is clear and original. All of the key concepts of the geography activity are included. This project is powerful and allows others to understand the main concepts.

Comments: _____

_____

❷ This geography project demonstrates an acceptable level of understanding of the key concepts. At least four themes of geography are presented appropriately. The visual aid is neat and colorful. Most words are spelled correctly, and the writing is acceptable even though there are some simple grammatical errors. Most of the key concepts of the geography activity are included. This project is acceptable and demonstrates that the student has gained knowledge about the key concepts.

Comments: _____

_____

❶ This geography project demonstrates a limited understanding of the key concepts. Only one or two of the five themes of geography are presented. The visual aid is unclear and not very neat. There are many spelling and grammatical errors. Few of the key concepts of the geography activity are included. This project is poor and demonstrates a lack of understanding of the main concepts. Revision is needed.

Comments: _____

_____

Five Themes Plate Rubric

(pages 68-70)

Name: _____ Class: _____

Project Title: ___*Five Themes Plate*___ Date: _____

Grading Scale: This geography project will receive a score of 4, 3, 2, or 1 to describe the effort, amount of knowledge, and degree of understanding demonstrated in its completion.

❹ This Five Themes Plate demonstrates a complete understanding of the key concepts. All five themes of geography are presented most proficiently. The Five Themes Plate is neat, colorful, and exceptionally attractive. All words are spelled correctly, and the plate is very original in design. All of the key concepts of the Five Themes Plate activity are included. The project is powerful and helps others understand how the five themes apply.

Comments: _____

❸ This Five Themes Plate demonstrates an adequate understanding of the key concepts. All five themes of geography are presented adequately. The Five Themes Plate is neat, colorful, and attractive. Most of the words are spelled correctly; the plate is original in design. Most of the key concepts of the Five Themes Plate activity are included. The project is impressive and helps others understand how the five themes apply.

Comments: _____

❷ This Five Themes Plate demonstrates a partial understanding of the key concepts. Three or four of the five themes of geography are presented. The Five Themes Plate is neat and colorful. Most of the words are spelled correctly. Most of the key concepts of the Five Themes Plate activity are included. The project is adequate and demonstrates that the student has gained some knowledge of how the five themes apply.

Comments: _____

❶ This Five Themes Plate demonstrates little or no understanding of the key concepts. One or two of the five themes of geography are presented. The Five Themes Plate is colorful, but not very neat. There are many spelling and grammatical errors. Few of the key concepts of the Five Themes Plate activity are included. The project is poor and demonstrates a lack of understanding of how the five themes apply. Revision is needed.

Comments: _____

Four-Point General Rubric

Name: _____ Class: _____

Project Title: _____ Date: _____

Grading Scale: This project will receive a score of 4, 3, 2, or 1 to describe the effort, amount of knowledge, and degree of understanding demonstrated in its completion.

④ Exemplary Achievement

- Demonstrates an exceptional understanding of major concepts.

- Communication is clear and shows originality.

- The visual is neat, colorful, and impressive.

③ Commendable Achievement

- Demonstrates an adequate understanding of major concepts.

- Communication is effective.

- The visual is neat and colorful.

② Limited Achievement

- Demonstrates a partial understanding of major concepts.

- Communication is somewhat ineffective.

- The visual is colorful.

① Little Achievement

- Demonstrates little understanding of major concepts.

- Communication is poor.

- The visual is not neat.

Self-Evaluation Rubric

Name: _____ Class: _____

Project Title: _____ Date: _____

Rating Scale:
😊 Excellent 😐 Satisfactory ☹️ Needs Improvement

Directions: At the end of each line, circle the face that best describes your work.

1. My work is neat, colorful, and organized.   😊   😐   ☹️

2. All words are spelled correctly.   😊   😐   ☹️

3. I used all five themes of geography.   😊   😐   ☹️

4. My work is original. I did not copy another person's work.   😊   😐   ☹️

5. I put my best effort into this project.   😊   😐   ☹️

Personal Statements:

6. The best part of this project was_____

_____.

7. My least favorite part of this project was _____

_____.

8. If I were the teacher, next time I would _____

_____.

9. Next time, I could do even better if I _____

_____.

Project Presentation Rubric

Name: _____ Class: _____

Project Title: _____ Date: _____

Grading Scale: This presentation will receive a score of 5, 4, 3, 2, or 1 to describe the effort, amount of knowledge, and degree of understanding demonstrated.

Main Elements of an Excellent Project Presentation:

- Speaks clearly and distinctly
- Demonstrates a clear understanding of the topic
- Explains how the project is related to the topic
- Gives accurate details and explanations of key points
- Answers questions related to the topic

❺ Outstanding	All five elements are evident to a high degree.
❹ Above Average	All five elements are evident.
❸ Satisfactory	Four of the elements are evident, or five are evident to some degree.
❷ Limited	Three of the elements are evident, or four are evident to some degree.
❶ Unsatisfactory	Only one or two of the elements are evident, or most are not done well.

Class-Created Rubric

Name: _____   Class: _____

Project Title: _____   Date: _____

Grading Scale: This project will receive a score of 5, 4, 3, 2, or 1 to describe the effort, amount of knowledge, and degree of understanding demonstrated.

Rubric Ranking	Description of Ranking
5	
4	
3	
2	
1	

Comments: _____

_____

_____

_____

Cause and Effect Diagram

Directions: Use this diagram to show the connection between a cause and the resulting effects. Write the cause in the sun and the resulting effects in the four connecting clouds.

Flag Graphic Organizer

Directions: After researching one of the original 13 U.S. colonies, use the colonial flag below to organize your information. Note that any shape can be used to organize facts about a topic.

Location   Place   Human/Environment Interaction   Movement   Regions

Coat of Arms Graphic Organizer

Directions: Research a U.S. city or state. Complete the graphic organizer using the five themes of geography as they relate to the place you researched.

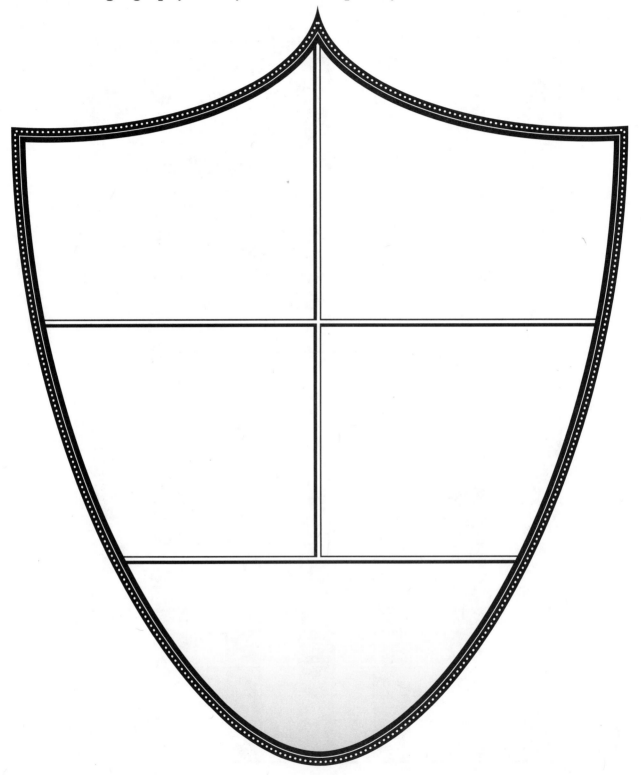

History Human Graphic Organizer

Directions: After researching a U.S. president, Native American, explorer, or patriot, complete the graphic organizer below.

National Geography Standards

Following are the National Geography Standards as written by the National Council for Geographic Education.* According to the standards, the geographically informed person knows and understands:

The World in Spatial Terms

1. How to use maps and other geographic representations, tools, and technologies to acquire, process, and report information from a spatial perspective.

2. How to use mental maps to organize information about people, places, and environments in a spatial context.

3. How to analyze the spatial organization of people, places, and environments on the earth's surface.

Places and Regions

4. The physical and human characteristics of places.

5. That people create regions to interpret the earth's complexity.

6. How culture and experience influence people's perceptions of places and regions.

Physical Systems

7. The physical processes that shape the patterns of the earth's surface.

8. The characteristics and spatial distribution of ecosystems on the earth's surface.

Human Systems

9. The characteristics, distribution, and migration of human populations on the earth's surface.

10. The characteristics, distribution, and complexity of the earth's cultural mosaics.

11. The patterns and networks of economic interdependence on the earth's surface.

12. The processes, patterns, and functions of human settlement.

13. How the forces of cooperation and conflict among people influence the division and control of the earth's surface.

Environment and Society

14. How human actions modify the physical environment.

15. How physical systems affect human systems.

16. The changes that occur in the meeting, use, distribution, and importance of resources.

The Uses of Geography

17. How to apply geography to interpret the past.

18. How to apply geography to interpret the present and plan for the future.

*Source: National Council for Geographic Education, http://www.ncge.org (accessed June 2005).

Answer Key

Page 8
Drawings will vary.

Page 9
1. road, 2. lake, 3. bridge, 4. school, 5. capital,
6. mountains, 7. city, 8. airport, 9. railroad,
10. highway, 11. forest, 12. river, 13. Reuben,
14. Kelsey and Cindy, 15. Randy,
16. northwest, 17. Adams, 18. Sam

Page 11
1. 100 mi., 2. 175 mi., 3. 320 km, 4. Menlo
River, 5. 300 mi., 6. 700 mi., 7. ⋀

Page 12
1. B-1, 2. C-6, 3. A-3 and A-4, 4. Ida Bank,
5. D-6, C-6, B-6

Page 13
1. Anna Island, 2. Map Key, 3. 25 mi.,
4. northwest, 5. northwest, 6. river,
7. Annabell

Page 14
1. location, 2. regions, 3. human/environment
interaction, 4. place, 5. movement

Page 15
1. 30°N, 2. 40°N, 3. 40°N, 4. 40°N, 5. 30°N, 6. 40°N

Page 16
1. Denver, 2. New Orleans and Memphis,
3. 80°W, 4. 95°W, 5. Philadelphia, 6. 93°W

Page 17
1. C., 2. B., 3. A., 4. D.

Page 18
1. Kentucky, Tennessee, Mississippi,
Alabama, Virginia, 2. Mississippi, 3. Texas,
Oklahoma, Arkansas, Louisiana, 4. Arkansas,
Oklahoma, Kansas, Colorado, 5. Columbia,
6. Illinois, Indiana, Ohio, West Virginia,
Kentucky, Pennsylvania, New York,
7. Colorado, Utah, Arizona, Nevada,
California, 8. Platte, 9. Missouri, Kansas,
Nebraska, Iowa, South Dakota, Montana,
Wyoming, North Dakota, 10. Colorado,
New Mexico, Texas, 11. Snake

Page 20
1. Appalachian Mountains, 2. Rocky
Mountains, 3. Chihuahuan, Sonoran, Mojave,
Great Basin, 4. Death Valley, California,
5. Mount McKinley, Alaska, 6. western,
7. Nevada, 8. Oklahoma, Michigan, Florida,
Maine, 9. east

Page 22
1. Texas, Southern Plains, 2. South Dakota,
Northern Plains, 3. Missouri, Northern
Plains, 4. New York, Northeastern,
5. Wyoming, Mountain, 6. California, Pacific,
7. Arizona, Mountain

Page 23

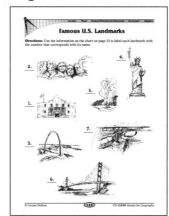

Page 25
Answers will vary for the state listings.
1. cattle, 2. citrus, 3. corn, 4. peanuts, 5.
cotton, 6. timber, 7. chickens, 8. sugar cane,
9. pigs

Page 27
1. 2,077, 2. 2,543, 3. 1,455, 4. 1,023, 5. 650,
6. 251, 7. 473, 8. 2,211, 9. 1,028, 10. 1,110

Page 28
1. Answers will vary. 2. 2:00 P.M., 3. Pacific,
4. 5:00 P.M., 5. Central, 6. 2 hrs., 7. 8:00 A.M.

Answer Key

Page 60
1. North Carolina, **2.** Vermont, **3.** Idaho,
4. Missouri, **5.** South Dakota, **6.** Hawaii,
7. Rhode Island, **8.** Maine, **9.** Alabama,
10. Iowa, **11.** Wyoming, **12.** New Mexico,
13. Georgia, **14.** California, **15.** Indiana,
16. Kansas, **17.** Nebraska, **18.** Connecticut,
19. Florida, **20.** Utah, **21.** Texas, **22.** Alaska,
23. Michigan, **24.** Nevada

Page 61
25. Washington, **26.** North Dakota,
27. Illinois, **28.** Wisconsin, **29.** Delaware,
30. Virginia, **31.** Colorado, **32.** Arizona,
33. Maryland, **34.** Tennessee, **35.** Louisiana,
36. Arkansas, **37.** South Carolina,
38. Montana, **39.** Pennsylvania, **40.** New York,
41. Mississippi, **42.** New Hampshire,
43. Massachusetts, **44.** Kentucky,
45. West Virginia, **46.** Oregon,
47. New Jersey, **48.** Minnesota, **49.** Oklahoma,
50. Ohio

Page 62
1. (Alabama) Southeastern, **2.** (Alaska)
Pacific, **3.** (Arizona) Mountain, **4.** (Arkansas)
Southern Plains, **5.** (California) Pacific,
6. (Colorado) Mountain, **7.** (Florida)
Southeastern, **8.** (Georgia) Southeastern,
9. (Hawaii) Pacific, **10.** (Illinois) Midwest,
11. (Kentucky) Southeastern, **12.** (Maryland)
Northeastern, **13.** (Massachusetts)
Northeastern, **14.** (Missouri) Northern
Plains, **15.** (Montana) Mountain,
16. (Nevada) Mountain, **17.** (New Jersey)
Northeastern, **18.** (New York) Northeastern,
19. (North Carolina) Southeastern,
20. (North Dakota) Northern Plains,
21. (Pennsylvania) Northeastern,
22. (Rhode Island) Northeastern,
23. (South Carolina) Southeastern,
24. (South Dakota) Northern Plains,
25. (Tennessee) Southeastern,
26. (Arizona, Colorado, Idaho, Montana,
Nevada, New Mexico, Utah, Wyoming)
Mountain, **27.** (Utah) Mountain,
28. (Virginia) Southeastern,

Page 62 continued
29. (Washington) Pacific, **30.** (West Virginia)
Southeastern, **31.** (Wyoming) Mountain,
32. (New York) Northeastern,
33. (Pennsylvania) Northeastern,
34. (Washington) Pacific,
35. (Alabama, Connecticut, Georgia,
Kentucky, Maine, Massachusetts, Maryland,
New Hampshire, New Jersey, New York,
North Carolina, Pennsylvania, Tennessee,
Vermont, Virginia, West Virginia),
Northeastern and Southeastern **36.** (Texas)
Southern Plains, **37.** (Wyoming) Mountain,
38. (Florida) Southeastern, **39.** (South
Carolina) Southeastern, **40.** (Ohio) Midwest

Page 104
1. Virginia, Massachusetts, Maryland,
Connecticut, Pennsylvania, **2.** Georgia,
Delaware, New Hampshire, Rhode Island,
3. Delaware, Virginia, **4.** Connecticut,
Delaware, Maryland, Virginia,
Massachusetts, New Hampshire, New York,
Rhode Island, **5.** Connecticut, Delaware,
Maryland, Rhode Island, Pennsylvania,
6. Connecticut, Georgia, Maryland, New
Hampshire, New Jersey, New York,
Pennsylvania, Rhode Island, **7.** Maryland,
Massachusetts, Virginia

Page 108
1. D., **2.** A., **3.** C., **4.** A., **5.** D.

Page 114
1. 10-12 feet, **2.** axle assembly, **3.** cotton
or canvas, **4.** prairie schooner, **5.** frame of
hickory bows, **6.** wheels, axle assembly,
reach, **7.** tar and tallow, **8.** jockey box,
9. drawstrings, **10.** Answers will vary.
11. Answers will vary.